Careful
OLD LETTERS

Careful
OLD LETTERS

A Jewish Family's Story
Lodz—Warsaw—Paris

ALEXANDRA WEINBAUM

Printed in the United States of America.

Cover design by Kerry Tinger
Book design by Colin Rolfe

ISBN: 978-1-963068-31-3 (sc)
ISBN: 978-1-963068-32-0 (e)

Library of Congress Control Number: 2024906742

Contents

Preface

In February 1996, shortly after my mother died, my son found a small carton labeled *Careful Old Letters*. It had been left behind in her storage locker. Had my son not noticed it, the box would have gone into the trash.

The box, which was coming apart at the seams, was filled with yellowing letters and postcards. On closer inspection, I saw that some of these letters and postcards were stamped with Nazi eagles and swastikas and had as the return address Litzmannstadt, the German name for the Polish city of Lodz, which Germany occupied in October 1939. Lodz was my parents' birthplace and home until they emigrated to the U.S. in 1938 at the ages of 28 and 30, and the place where my grandmother died in the Lodz Ghetto, and the place from which other relatives were transported to Auschwitz.

Still mourning my mother's death following her seven-year illness, I was not up to finding out more about the box's contents. When I eventually examined the contents, I found that among the letters were 39 postcards from the Lodz Ghetto. They were from my maternal grandmother, Mera Rozin, written in German, the first in May 1940 and the last in June 1941. I assumed my grandmother used German because that would allow the letters to more easily pass the Nazi censors. That my grandmother was able to write in German did not surprise me since she studied German in school and spoke and read it fluently.

As a child, I knew something about one of the two survivors from our family. My father's first cousin Dosia lived with us for a short time after she came to the United States in 1947 when I was five years old. Eventually, I came to have a blurry sense that she survived something terrible. I saw numbers tattooed on her arm, which she covered with a Band-aid. I also sensed that she was treated with special concern and tenderness by my father.

The only other concrete piece of information I had about family members' fates was a postcard that my parents kept in the family album. When I was eleven, they translated and read it to me. It was from my grandmother, written from the Lodz Ghetto, and it contained a list of all the things she needed — tea, coffee, powdered milk, cooking oil, canned goods, bedding, a nightgown, sweaters, blankets, scissors, Nivea Creme. The list of such basic necessities made a deep impression on me, but I never discussed its implications with my parents.

My parents and I rarely talked about their families and especially not about their fate in World War II. Nor did they tell me that there were many other letters and "postcards" from my grandmother and from other relatives and friends that I might want to know about some day. My grandmother was for me unknown except for several photos in the family album, along with stories that my mother shared with me from her own childhood.

Several months after finding the box of letters, I decided to look for someone who could translate the postcards from my grandmother. A close friend told me her German neighbor might be able to help. Tom Sauermilch is married to an Israeli woman, Ida Barak, whose parents were from Krakow and survived the war. Tom and Ida met when they were both students at Indiana University. Tom, who is not Jewish, immediately volunteered to translate the postcards. We worked in my fourth floor study during five hot nights in July 1997. Tom translated the postcards into English while I sat at the computer. He never said a word about the contents except to explain a confusing phrase or sentence.

And this respectful silence was a gift to me. What could he say? He barely knew me or my family history, and the contents were so desperately sad. Cries for help, pleas for food packages and for more letters, and barely concealed despair in reporting that the packages my parents sent arrived crushed and useless.

I told people about the postcards and photocopied the translations for my children. Everyone said I must do something with the rest of the letters, but I didn't for many years. The fact that I was working full-time was a ready excuse, but I know that the reasons were more complex. My grandmother's "postcards" opened a window not only into who she was but also into what my parents must have felt as they received postcard after postcard and letter after letter from other relatives and friends some from the Warsaw Ghetto and some from France where my parents lived for 10 years while my father completed medical school and an internship and residency in ophthalmology. I also imagined how they must have felt when there were no more postcards from my grandmother after June 12, 1941, and finally at the end of the war, when they knew that none of their parents, nor anyone else in the family, had survived except for Dosia and her brother Adek.

When I retired in the beginning of 2009, I returned to the letters. I opened *Careful — Old Letters* and found letters from my parents' friends with names I recognized; letters from the two survivors, Dosia and Adek, for whom my parents obtained visas to the U.S in 1947; many long letters from my grandmother Mera to my parents after they emigrated to the U.S. in April 1938 and before the war began; and even one letter from my grandmother dated September 1, 1939, the day the Germans invaded Poland. There were also letters from the Warsaw Ghetto from my paternal grandparents, Roza and Aron Wolkowicz, with a few brief words in Polish hiding their desperation and anguish.

There were love letters between my parents who were students in France where they met and fell in love. When my mother returned to Lodz for the summer in 1930, they corresponded weekly — she then 22 and my father 20. From November 1931 through May 1932, my mother returned to Poland because neither she nor her parents had the means to send her back to the university to study. During this period apart, they corresponded regularly.

And there were letters from Julius Love, my mother's grand uncle who sponsored my parents' emigration to the U.S. in 1938, thereby saving them and making my life possible. By 1938, my parents knew that their futures as "foreign Israelites," as they were known in the French bureaucracy, were uncertain, and life in Poland was terrible both from an economic perspective and because of increased anti-Semitism in the late thirties. Reluctantly, and at the last possible moment, they accepted the offer of Uncle Love, as they called him, to sponsor them and provide visas because it was the "rational" thing to do. They must have thought that they, in turn, would bring their parents to the States over time.

In total, the carton contained 169 letters and postcards in German and Polish, and a few in Russian and French. To find translators, I first went to the Center for Jewish History in New York City. However, the people on their list told me they only translated documents because letters were too difficult and time consuming. I then called the Polish Cultural Institute whose director put me in touch with a faculty member from the Slavic department at Columbia University. This was Anna Frajlich, a Polish poet, whose book of poems, *Between Dawn and the Wind*, written after her parents were forced to leave Poland in 1968 as a result of the anti-Semitic campaigns of the government, has become a treasured volume.

Anna referred me to her graduate student, Elizabeth Kosakowska, who agreed to translate the letters written in Polish and Russian before the war by my maternal grandmother and grandfather, Mera and Sasha, and the letters from friends and other relatives. The German postcards, although already translated by Tom, were still in a first stage of translation. Elizabeth referred me to her colleague in Virginia, Agnieszka McClure, to translate the German postcards from my grandmother. Both Elizabeth and Agnieszka are experienced translators who had worked for the Holocaust Museum in Washington, DC. In addition to the German postcards, Agnieszka translated all of my parents' letters to one another from 1930 to 1932.

I am tremendously grateful to both Elizabeth and Agnieszka. They were confronted with many challenges: deciphering so many different handwritings; researching historically specific references to films, books, and political events; and translating proverbs from Russian or Yiddish. They captured the consistency of voice across individual writers' letters, especially my parents' voices.

What was most difficult for me was the thought that I was sharing letters with people I barely knew, letters that contained some of the most intimate and terrible moments in the lives of my family. I wondered what Elizabeth and Agnieszka thought about them and what they might say to me. Sometimes they would comment on the letters—the gentleness of my grandfather, Sasha ("what a nice man he must have been")—the emotionality and liveliness of my grandmother's letters before the war, and the romance of my parents' love letters. I am forever grateful to the two women for their sensitivity and respect for my feelings as well as the feelings of those writing in desperate times.

When the translations came I read them eagerly, but I was not able to take in much of what I read—not immediately. It was as if I had met someone for the first time, but this person at our first meeting revealed the most vulnerable and desperate side of their life. It took time to understand the letters, to go beyond the surface meaning to the situation that led to their writing. A letter from the Warsaw Ghetto in which my mother's uncle Artek says "we have nothing" and his son Marchelek "is doing poorly and no longer goes to school" masks a historical setting about which I now know a great deal—a starvation diet, no work for his parents, who are scrounging to keep their son alive —a setting much more horrible than the simple words could possibly convey. And I know the ending of the story: Marchelek and his parents died in the Warsaw Ghetto or in Treblinka. I cannot imagine myself in that place and time nor how I would have acted as a parent.

But beyond this challenge of taking in the meaning of what words were insufficient to convey, there is something else: my parents, in this respect like Holocaust survivors, tried to "close the book" on their relatives' experiences during the Holocaust because it was too painful to reopen. Eva Hoffman writes that for children of survivors, the Shoah is a kind of mythology: "We receive the knowledge of terrible events with only childish instruments of perception, and as a kind of fable."[1] Parents who survived discouraged curiosity, because in Hoffman's words, "to be curious was to uncover the unspeakable." My parents felt the taboo of talking about those who perished, because of their entire family only two others survived besides themselves. This is one of the reasons that I delayed delving into *Careful Old Letters*. As a child I too wasn't explicitly told "not to ask" but I too "knew it in my bones." And reading the letters as an adult, I experienced that curb on my curiosity, the taboo against opening old wounds.

Slowly, glacially slowly, I have let the writers of these letters into my heart and life, and I have learned to accept them as they are on the page—from before the war when they are ordinary people going about their lives, having children, worrying about business—to later, writing in desperation, trying to emigrate and pleading with my parents to help them. I know the writers of these letters in ways that are unimaginable in normal times. I have peopled my memory with their names, with their handwriting, with their idiosyncratic expressions, and sometimes with faces, known from the many photographs of the letter writers from before the war. I have tried in these pages to "carefully" give voice to people from our family, so that the box my father kept and labeled was not preserved in vain.

Endnotes

1 Hoffman, *After Such Knowledge: Memory, History, and the Legacy of the Holocaust*, 16.

Chapter 1

Childhood and Leaving Home—
From Lodz to Grenoble, 1908–1929

Growing up, Halina Rozin and Mikhal Izrael Wolkowicz, who would become my parents, lived only six blocks from one another in Lodz. Their apartments were located on Gdanska and Grodmiejska Streets, just off the main fashionable street in Lodz, Piotrkowska. Today the street is lined with shops, cafes, and whimsical statues of Lodz's famous artists, writers, and textile magnates. The statues of Jewish historical figures are a contemporary celebration of what was once a diverse and wealthy city. But the prewar Jewish population of 200,000 is now reduced to about 300. And on the streets just beyond Piotrkowska poverty is evident, as are occasional racist and anti-Semitic graffiti on buildings and billboards.

The city, whose name means "small boat," was established in the nineteenth century and bore the name of a nearby village. By the last quarter of the nineteenth century Lodz had become the "Manchester of Poland," a major textile center, specializing in the production of cotton clothing for the vast Russian market. Because many Jews were in trades and commerce related to making and selling clothing, they settled in the city in large numbers.

While the city produced great wealth through its textile factories, most of the Jewish and Polish residents were impoverished workers. Baluty, the poorest area of Lodz, became the site of the Lodz Ghetto during World War II. Before the war it was home to a large and poor Jewish population––shopkeepers, peddlers, shoemakers, carpenters, and tailors. But the contrast in wealth among the Jewish population was huge. The largest textile factory was owned by Izrael K. Poznanski, the Jewish textile magnate represented in the sculpture on Piotrkowska Street. His complex of factory buildings on Piotrkowska as well as a residence built to look like an eighteenth century palace surrounded by gardens has now been converted into a museum and park that is a focal point for tourists.

Before World War I Poland did not exist. It was divided among the Russian, German, and Austro-Hungarian Empires in the last quarter of the eighteenth century. Despite the heroic uprising in Warsaw in 1863 to overthrow Russian rule and subsequent attempts to gain local power during the revolution of 1905, what was once the Polish Kingdom remained firmly controlled from Vienna, Berlin, and Moscow until November 1918. At this time, Polish politicians and generals took advantage of the impending defeat of the German and Austro-Hungarian Empires, as well as the Russian Revolution, and declared Poland an independent country.

Lodz grew rapidly in the interwar period and by 1931 was a city of close to 600,000, of which 59 percent were Polish, 32 percent Jewish, and 9 percent German.[1] Middle and upper middle class Jews like my grandparents and their siblings were involved in the textile industry and commerce but also participated in other professions: teaching, medicine, dentistry, law, social work, and engineering. While most Jews in the newly independent Poland spoke Yiddish as their primary language, they also knew Polish, Russian, and German, and often spoke all three as "second" languages which allowed them to carry on their business affairs.

My Mother's Family

Mera and Alexander Rozin, my maternal grandparents

My mother's father, Alexander Rozin (for whom I am named), was born in Moscow in 1882 but spent much of his youth in Lodz, where his father Azriel and mother Sara had nine children, he being the eldest. The fact that my great grandfather was a merchant in Moscow before the revolution speaks to his economic status since Jewish merchants were only allowed to live in Moscow if they were wealthy. The Rozin family's upper middle class status was affirmed when I visited the Lodz Jewish Cemetery in search of my grandfather's grave and those of his parents. The graves were located in the same area of the cemetery as the grand mausoleum erected by Poznanski, the textile magnate. Our guide told me that my great grandparents must have been wealthy because this part of the cemetery had the most expensive grave sites.[2]

My grandfather always known by his nickname, Sasha was a secular, assimilated Jew. He never went to synagogue although my grandmother did, but on her own, and only on the high holidays. My mother followed in her father's footsteps. She went to her paternal grandparents' Passover seders, but beyond this had no Jewish upbringing or understanding of the important Jewish holidays. My mother's family was not kosher, and they spoke Russian or Polish at home, not Yiddish, although they certainly knew it. Later my parents often used Yiddish expressions for emphasis and humor but in the typical fashion of assimilated Jews of their time referred to the language as "jargon."

While this attitude seems supercilious, it was prevalent in the mid-nineteenth-to -twentieth century among Jews who chose assimilation and embraced the Polish language and culture. In the latter part of the nineteenth century, assimilation among upper middle class Polish Jews grew rapidly. This meant emancipation of women and men from early, arranged marriages as well as a secular education for girls equivalent to that of boys.

My mother's mother, Mera Kagan, is a good example of such assimilation. She was born in 1884 in Suwalki, a medium-sized city in the Russian part of Poland,[3] but she grew up in Lodz where she attended a rigorous German gymnasium. By the time she graduated from the gymnasium, she read, wrote, and spoke German fluently. Her best friend in school was Tania, my grandfather's oldest sister, who introduced her to my grandfather. Mera and Sasha fell in love and shortly after my grandmother graduated were married in Lodz in 1904 at the ages of 20 and 22. Their wedding announcement was written in German, suggesting the multilingual world of the two families. My mother, Halina Rozin, was born in 1908 in Lodz.

My maternal grandmother Mera Kagan with her sister Dora and brother Jacob circa 1903

Moving to Moscow

A few years later, the family moved to Moscow, where my grandfather managed a cigarette factory, a position which his father had made possible. My mother remembered a spacious apartment and a nanny who frequently took her along to church. She recalled being awed by the beauty of the Russian Orthodox church and music.

My mother was nine years old when the Bolsheviks easily overthrew the government, then under the leadership of Alexander Kerensky, and established a Soviet Republic in November 1917, promising "bread, land and peace" to a devastated country and starving populace. Her memories of this period were vivid. She remembered that the factory where her father was a manager was, like all factories, given to the workers' committee to control and manage, but the workers chose to keep him as manager. They trusted and liked my grandfather.

During the early years of the Soviet Republic, the living conditions of the middle and upper classes deteriorated dramatically and quickly. My grandparents' apartment was subdivided with curtains separating each living quarter, and everyone shared a communal kitchen. My grandfather, who was in fragile health because of a chronic heart condition, became very sick. Food was scarce and access to medical care impossible. My mother recalled that at school each child was given a hard-boiled egg to provide nourishment in scarce times. She hid and saved the egg for her father and told her parents that she had been given an "extra" egg. She also remembered the revolutionary children's songs which she learned in school.

Returning to Lodz

In late 1918 or early 1919, my grandparents, Mera and Sasha, and my mother, Halina (Galina in Russian), moved back to Lodz. Their greatly curtailed living conditions, along with my grandfather's failing health, must have influenced the decision to return. The decision was also affected by Poland's status as an independent republic beginning in November 1918.[4] Although leftist in his politics, my grandfather was not a Bolshevik supporter. Nevertheless, he was a personal acquaintance of Grigory Zinoviev, a leader in the Bolshevik Party. According to my mother, Zinoviev helped arrange for my parents' passage back to Poland.

On the return trip to Poland, the family was met at the Polish border by the military police, who immediately arrested my grandfather, claiming that he was a spy for the Soviet Union. Another man on the train was seized for the same reason. According to my mother, my grandmother saved my grandfather's life. She confronted the officer, and told him that her husband was suffering from ill health. She said he needed medical attention, which he could not get in the Soviet Union, and that he was returning to his family in Lodz.

She also told the officer that he was anti-Semitic in assuming that her husband was a spy for the Soviet government simply because he was Jewish, which the officer knew from his passport. The association between Jews and Communists already had a strong and negative association in Poland, as in the Polish characterization of all Jews as, "Zydo-Komuna" (Jew/Communist). The use of the term "was a two edged sword, which used old and wide- spread anti-Jewish feelings in order to discredit the communists and at the same time used anti-Boshevik feelings to justify anti-Semitism. The term Zydo-Komuna seemed particularly manipulative and useful, since it joined together old stereotypes and brand new ones."[5]

The incident was not unique. Anti-Semitic incidents and pogroms were happening in selected Polish cities and towns, especially in the period immediately after wartime hostilities ended in 1918. It is not clear why the officer relented when he heard my grandmother's passionate advocacy for her husband's life. The other man arrested on the train was given a summary hearing and shot as a spy. The heart of the story for my mother was her mother's courage in speaking truth to brute power and prejudice.

Not voiced in my mother's recounting of the story was her own trauma as a child in witnessing this moment in her parents' lives. My mother, like her mother, was not afraid to speak out against injustice. She was also certain that the worst could happen at any moment—and for good reason, beginning with her family's entry into Poland. My father affectionately called her "djadja neschastie," a Russian term meaning "uncle disaster." This childhood traumatic incident left its mark on her psyche throughout her life.

At the time of the family's return to Lodz to join the rest of their relatives, Lodz was the second largest city in an independent Polish Republic, in which Poles, Jews, Ukrainians, Lithuanians, Germans, and Belorussians were now living together in a democratic state. After Poland was internationally recognized as an independent republic under the Versailles Treaty, the allies developed a Minorities Treaty to address the rights of minorities in the newly created republic. Their concerns stemmed especially from the outbreak of anti-Semitic incidents at the end of the war. The treaty required that minorities in Poland be assured of equal protection under the law and that the equality of all citizens of the republic was guaranteed regardless of differences in nationality, religion, or language. Within Poland all of the minority groups, of which Jews were the second largest after the Ukrainians, welcomed what was at the time a very progressive document. However, many Poles saw it as something imposed by the Western powers, and over time, when nationalist, antidemocratic parties were ascendant in the thirties, it was honored more in the breach than in practice. Because my maternal grandparents returned as citizens of the former Russian Empire, they had to apply for Polish citizenship, which was granted in 1920. My mother Halina regretted leaving a home that she loved in Moscow and refused to speak Polish. As a result, she lost time in school and was a grade behind her age cohort. She was eventually enrolled in a private girls' Catholic school in which there were four other Jewish students. According to Polish law (and this still applies in Poland), religious education had to be provided in schools, whether they were state run or private. In my mother's school a rabbi came once a week to provide religious instruction for the five girls, a training which clearly did not "count" and to which Halina paid absolutely no attention. In fact, this mandatory instruction was often led by incompetent clergy, and since it didn't count as a subject, provided an opportunity for mischief and mayhem.

By her own account a "mischievous" kid, Halina was likely to have been one of the ring leaders when pranks occurred. She was not an outstanding student except in the subjects she loved French and Polish literature. However, by the time she graduated with her matura, the highest degree offered by a gymnasium and equivalent to our high school plus two years of college, she spoke French fluently, wrote it well, and was well educated in classic Polish literature.

In Lodz, she grew up surrounded by a large, close-knit family. Her aunt Dora, whose son Adek was like a younger brother for my mother, lived nearby. Her paternal grandparents lived so close that my mother went to their apartment daily to practice the piano. Friday dinners, and of course seders seating 40, at her grandparents' apartment were part of her life growing up. Two of her uncles on her father's side, Lolek and Fredek, were only six and seven years older than she was. She was very close to both of them and told me how important they were in her late adolescence, often as escorts to parties and places where she could not go alone.

Unlike her father's parents, her mother's family was observant. A story my mother told me suggested the divide that occurred after her mother, Mera, married a secular Jewish man. One evening Mera's father, Josel Marosz, came to dinner and suddenly announced when the main course was served that he could not eat the food because it was not kosher. He was visibly angry, feeling that his daughter had tried to fool him, got up from the table, and said he was leaving. His daughter persuaded him to stay, explaining that the carrots which he thought were cooked in butter were, in fact, cooked in margarine, and she reassured him that the meal, the dishes, and the preparation were kosher. Clearly, my grandmother followed her in-laws' secular ways but also accommodated her father's need for kosher meals.

I was amazed by one aspect of my grandfather Sasha's family: how politically engaged four of my grandfather's eight siblings were. His three sisters, Pepa, Nunia, and Tania became Communists, married Communists, and went to live in the Soviet Union before the war, and his second youngest brother, Lolek, was high up in the Polish Communist Party.

Although the number of Jews in the Polish Communist Party (PPK) during the interwar years was small (approximately 9,000 members), Jews constituted about 20 percent of party members—a very high percentage given that they were only 9 percent of the overall population.[6] Membership in the party came primarily from middle class assimilated Jews, like my grandfather's family. The attraction for Jews was certainly the party's strong stance against anti-Semitism in Poland, as well as its identification with a Communist future that would erase religious, national, and class barriers. While opposing nationalism, whether Polish or Jewish as the basis for its politics, the Party nevertheless argued for the use of Yiddish and Jewish education. Over time, as the government embraced anti Semitic policies, the Party took a stance regarding proletarian internationalism "not as a cosmopolitan notion, but also allowing room for Jewish national existence."[7]

At some point, my mother's uncle Lolek was imprisoned for his political activities in the Party. Eventually he was traded for a Polish prisoner in the Soviet Union. Shortly after arriving in Russia he met his death along with all of the other Polish Communists in the purge carried out under Stalin's order. The independent stance of the Polish Communist Party was not tolerable to Stalin, and essentially the Party ceased to exist after 1938. My mother's antipathy to Stalin and, in general, to the Soviet Union was shaped by her loss of a favorite uncle.

Halina was also close to her aunts, especially Pepa. A dedicated teacher of poor children in the public schools, Pepa told Halina stories about her students. One story my mother liked to relate later was about a little boy who, when asked what his father did, said he was a "horse." Pepa asked him to explain, and he said "my father pulls a wagon so he is a horse." Pepa explained to the child that his father was a worker, and that all work was honorable and valuable.

Another story was that as a very young child, perhaps four or five, Halina heard her aunts speaking about poor children not having toys like hers. After listening for a while, she went to her room, gathered her favorite toys, and threw them out the window, hoping that poor children would find and enjoy them. This story always amused me not only because of my mother's "first political awakening" inspired by her Communist aunts but also because of her impulsivity, a trait which I knew well.

Tania, the eldest sister who introduced my grandparents, also went to the Soviet Union before World War II with her husband Henri, who is mentioned in my grandmother's letters from the Lodz Ghetto. He was able to send her food from the city of Riga in the Soviet Union until the Germans invaded Russia in 1941.

My grandfather Sasha had five brothers. Monek became a physician and died in 1920 fighting for Poland in the war with the Soviet Union, when the Poles fought under General Pilsudski. Janek became a lawyer who converted to Catholicism in order to be appointed a judge, a necessary condition for this position. He survived the war because of his conversion and corresponded with my parents after the war. The two youngest brothers were Fredek, an engineer, and Lolek, a gifted pianist before he became a committed Communist. Artek was especially close to my mother. He maintained a correspondence with her when she emigrated to the States and later when he, his wife, and young son were starving in the Warsaw Ghetto, he sent urgent pleas to her for help.[8]

My Father's Family

I know much less about my father's family because he was not immersed in a loving extended family like my mother's. In contrast to my mother, my father told me much more about his schooling and his friends. He remained close to those who survived the war throughout his life.

My paternal grandparents, Roza and Aron Wolkowicz, Lodz circa 1930

Aron Wolkowicz, my paternal grandfather, was born in Gombin in 1885.[9] He was also involved in the textile business and may have been a manager in the Poznanski factory. When my son Daniel visited Poland and found the apartment building in which my father lived on Gdanksa Street in Lodz, he was invited to see an apartment that was being renovated. When the woman showing him the apartment learned that his great grandfather lived in the building in the interwar period, she told him that the building originally was reserved for managers who worked for Poznanski. It is located close to the factory complex.

My father's grandmother, Ruchel Goldberg, lived in a shtetl; my father told me that she wore the traditional wig for married women and spoke Yiddish with her family. My father liked to make jokes about life in the shtetl, and especially about his grandmother. When my mother served a soup that he especially liked, he would lift the soup dish to his mouth, and slurp the last drop very noisily, announcing, "And now I am going to show you how Grandma Ruchel ate her soup."

Everyone in the family seemed to agree that my grandfather Aron was a kind and gentle man, who was completely overwhelmed and controlled by his wife. According to my father, his mother was a "hard" woman, practical, concerned with money and status, and fanatical about cleanliness, something that my father inherited from her.

In all other ways my father Mikhal was much more like his father. A story he liked to tell revealed his father's kindness and his mother's rigidity. As a child he begged for a bicycle, which his mother adamantly refused to give him, considering this a "goyish" and useless possession. His father secretly bought one for him and hid it where he could access it secretly.

Mikhal's life growing up in Lodz was shaped the most by his parents' choice of a school. Although they were less educated than Halina's parents, they chose a rigorous and modern school for their son, one which demonstrated their attention to education and their hopes that he would be well qualified to succeed in the new Polish republic.

In Poland, in addition to the public schools, which most Jewish children attended, there were several types of private schools that addressed the rights of Jews as stated by the Minorities Treaty. Jews and other minority groups were guaranteed the right to have schools that honored their language and culture.[10] The interwar period saw three types of Jewish schools in Poland: Cysho, which taught in Yiddish; Tarbut, which were bilingual in Polish and modern Hebrew, the kind Mikhal attended; and Orthodox and ultra- Orthodox.[11]

The Bilingual Hebrew-Polish Tarbut schools, one of which my father attended, originated in Lodz. The founding organization sponsored 13 schools, all girls' and all boys' schools as well as coeducational schools, some with concentrations on the humanities and others on mathematics and science. It embraced a Zionist philosophy and taught both modern Hebrew and Polish. In Lodz, 1,617 boys and 2,398 girls attended such schools in 1924.[12]

The school Mikhal attended, like the others, began in kindergarten and finished at a level that was the equivalent to the first two years of college in the U.S. Unlike the other Jewish private schools, this one alone entitled students who earned the matura to apply to a Polish University because these schools were not "political" in the same way that the Cysho schools were, nor religious, as the Orthodox and Ultra-Orthodox were. Mikhal attended a summer camp run by the school, where he learned to wrestle, play soccer, and run races.

My father's class photo in 1924. He is in second row, second from left, age 14

What mattered most in my father's life was the way his childhood friendships developed over the years and remained the most important ties in his life beyond our small family. Like my father, several of his friends went to France to study, and he remained in contact with them throughout his days in Paris. One, Bolek Bejslechem, his closest friend, survived the war in France, and afterwards they corresponded and eventually visited one another from the 1950s on.[13]

Another, Marek (Mark) Zborowski became a Communist at the age of 14, rose quite high up in the Party and later became an anthropologist and author.[14]

Leaving Poland for France

Although both of my parents attended schools that provided a matura, the degree they needed to gain entry to a Polish University, neither chose to attend a university in Poland. Perhaps they sought adventure and distance from their parents, much as students in the U.S. who can afford to go away to college do.

However, there may have been other reasons. As early as the late 1920s, an "unofficial" quota of student representation equal to their proportion in the population, which for Jews was between 9 and 10 percent, prevailed in some universities. This became officially sanctioned in the mid-thirties. Moreover, a number of universities had instituted "ghetto benches" where Jews were required to sit separately during lectures. Jewish students chose to stand rather than abide by this racist policy. Anti-Semitic thugs beat Jewish students who stood up to them in several cases, to death.[15]

My parents left before these events occurred. But clearly, like many other Polish Jews, their preference was to study in a country that since the French Revolution had accepted Jews as equal citizens and in the twentieth century welcomed Jewish immigrants from Eastern and Central Europe so much so that Jewish émigrés far outnumbered French-born Jews.[16]

Although my parents were neighbors in Lodz, their lives never intersected because of the great differences in their families' worlds. But they found each other anyway—this in the international student world of the University of Grenoble, where both chose to go initially. My father had already been there for a year in a pre-med program when he met my mother in the middle of his second year. By the time the semester ended, they had fallen in love.

A New Year photo from my father's school. He is in the last row, fourth from the left.

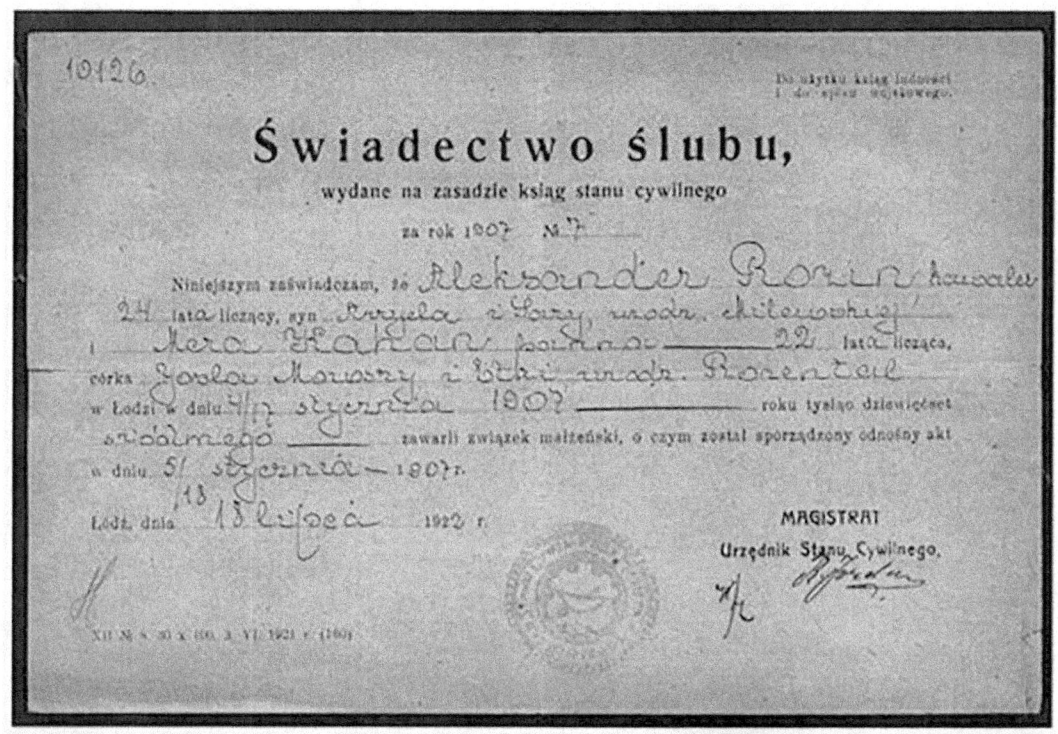

Marriage license for Alexander Rozin and Mera Kagan, January 1907

Birth certificate of Halina Rozin in Russian, April 22, 1908

Endnotes

1 This breakdown is based on first language preference, which for the majority of Jews would have been Yiddish. Horwitz, Ghettostadt: *Lodz and the Making of a Nazi City.*

2 The Lodz Cemetery was built in 1882 and comprised over 100 acres. It is the largest Jewish cemetery in Europe.

3 In the latter quarter of the nineteenth century it was town of over 20,000, the fourth largest in the Russian controlled part of Poland with a mixed Lithuanian and Jewish population that became even more diverse as it industrialized. http://en.wikipedia.org/wiki/Suwalki

4 Internationally, the state of Poland was not recognized until the Treaty of Versailles was signed on June 28, 1919.

5 Mishkinsky, "The Communist Party of Poland and Jews," *The Jews of Poland Between Two World Wars,* 66.

6 Mishkinsky, 62.

7 Ibid., 71.

8 When my mother and I created a family tree together, she told me the names of the five brothers, using their nicknames. I have not located the Lodz records which would give their full names.

9 Gombin was a shtetl about 90 miles from Warsaw. The population was two thirds Jewish, one third Polish, and had a small number of Germans. Jews probably spoke Yiddish most of the time but certainly knew Polish. Aron did not write in Polish but certainly spoke it. http://www.jewishgen.org/Yizkor/pinkas_poland/pol4_001 54.html

10 This right was ensured by the Minorities Treaty. Theoretically, a promise was also made to provide funding for schools that were established where minorities constituted 25 percent or more of the population, but this was not adequately fulfilled, particularly in relation to the Jewish schools. Eisenstein, *Jewish Schools in Poland* 1919-38, 20–26.

11 Ibid., 20-26.

12 Ibid., 70.

13 See Chapter 6, which is devoted to Bolek and his enduring friendship with my father.

14 See Chapter 2 for more information about Mark Zborowski.

15 Heller, *On the Edge of Destruction: Jews of Poland between the Two World Wars,* 125.

16 By 1940, immigrant Jews far outnumbered long- established Jews in France. There were 330,000 foreign Jews and 90,000 French-born. Poznanski, *Jews in France During World War II,* 1.

Chapter 2

Love Letters from Lodz, Grenoble, and Paris, 1928–1932

I have four photos of my parents as students: my mother's taken in 1930 in Lodz after she had completed her first year at the university; my father's taken in Paris in 1931, by then a medical student, wearing a jauntily slanted beret (see page 19); both parents, holding one another around the waist and peering out from under a tree, and a fourth in which my grandmother looks at my parents with longing because she knows they will leave soon to return to Paris where they have made their lives.

When I look at these photos I feel a longing for the world my parents lost. I have a sense—perhaps romanticized—of their lives enriched by close friends, warm family relationships, and hope for the future. Jump forward to 1945 when the war has ended, and by then almost everyone whom they knew and loved has perished. My parents were the lucky ones who left in time, and they rarely spoke of the world they left behind. In this chapter I have tried to resurrect their world from the letters they exchanged over a two- year period.

My mother gave her photo to my father after their whirlwind romance in Grenoble. On the back she wrote "*To Mish*" one of her many nicknames for my father "*from Hala, 1930.*" This is the earliest photo that I have of my mother. Our family album had many photos of my father from his babyhood on, and many photos of his high school girlfriend. But of my mother, not one photo remains until she became part of my father's life. It makes this photo all the more precious.

My mother sent this photo to my father in 1930

My parents in Kolumna circa 1934

The two photos of my parents together are from Kolumna, a Polish vacation town just outside of Lodz, where my mother's aunt Dora owned a vacation pension named for her, Pensionnat Dora. In the first photo my mother is wearing a lovely print summer blouse and high- heeled shoes. I cannot remember a time when my mother did not wear her heels, even in the country. In the second photo her dress reminds me of a historic photo, which I saw in 2012 enlarged to billboard size on one of the few remaining walls of what once was the Warsaw Ghetto. In it several young women in the 1930s enjoy a summer day in flowing print dresses and sandals as they walk gaily and boldly down Muranov Street in the Jewish section of town. Like these young women who "own" the street, I like to think of my parents in this moment as having confidence in themselves, in their futures, and in their mutual love for each other.

The letters that I quote were written between May and November 1930 and from November 1931 through May 1932. At the beginning of the correspondence, my parents had just turned 20 and 22, respectively, my father the younger of the two. After a whirlwind romance of several months in Grenoble where they were students, they separated during the vacation months. My mother, Halina, returned to her parents in Lodz and then returned to Grenoble in the fall.

From November 1931 to May 1932 my parents' correspondence resumed. By then my father had moved to Paris to continue his studies in medicine. My mother, who could not afford to return to the university, and had not taken her final exams, stayed with her parents during this time and took on odd jobs, mostly as a tutor in French. When she joined my father in Paris in May 1932, they remained together as a couple, although they did not marry until October 9, 1934.[1]

I begin with an explanation of the multitude of nicknames that my parents used for each other and a physical description of the letters. My mother called my father by an assortment of Polish nicknames—mainly *Mus* or *Musieniek*, occasionally *Mikhal*. My father had an unusually bold and large handwriting. If I had only his handwriting by which to judge his personality, I would guess he was someone with a great deal of confidence or the opposite, someone who was compensating for a lack of confidence. Reading the letters, I saw both sides of him his dependence on my mother for support and love to carry him through his medical studies, but also his boldness and steadfastness in pursuing opportunities related to his career in spite of obstacles. He looked for ways to learn and to support himself and never expressed a sense of defeat—only occasionally of physical exhaustion.

My father wrote on whatever pieces of paper were on hand. Once, he cried while writing and drew arrows pointing to the tear stains—hoping to prove his love and yearning for my mother. My mother who was also called by an assortment of nicknames, such as Hala, Halinka, Halinochka, and Halush, among others, had her own stationary, with the initial of her first name, Halina, imprinted in blue to match the blue-lined envelopes. She wrote in a small, neat hand.

My father's addresses in Paris kept changing. He moved from place to place within the fifth arrondissement, always close to the medical school and the Sorbonne, seeking lodgings with various roommates at an affordable rent. Most of the envelopes he used after he moved to Paris were from the Foyer des Etudiants Juifs[2] which sponsored the restaurant on Rue Latran where he worked as a waiter.

My mother wrote from two places: her family's apartment in Lodz on Grodmieska Street, where she grew up, and during the summer from a country-like suburb of Lodz, near a small lake.

I have read and reread their letters, trying to understand the passionate and sometimes troubled love between my mother and father. I have come to admire their strengths and understand how difficult their lives were. Money is a frequent topic in the letters. Both came from middle class families who had fallen on hard times. Neither family could afford to support their children's university education. For my father it meant going hungry at times and working long hours every day while also going to classes and studying.

My parents told me about the hard times and lack of money, but I never understood what that meant until I read the letters. Now I also understand better my father's drive and steadfast pursuit of his dream to be a physician, and how hard that was — working as a waiter many hours a week, taking courses, not having enough money for books, always, always worrying about money. He chose to struggle alone. He rarely returned home except for brief visits. His relationship with his mother was strained, and this comes through in his letters. However, unlike my mother he had many close friends.

My mother had similar concerns but, as a woman still embedded in a loving and extended family was more protected. She had a large family of grandparents, cousins, uncles and aunts, all living close by. She was close to many of her relatives, including her youngest uncles, among them especially Fredek, who was only a few years older than she was. It was difficult for her to leave her parents and this world of caring relatives, but once committed to my father she wanted to be only with him.

**Friends and my father, second from right. Friends include
Mark Zborowski (right, passing a card)**

After the letters were translated, one of my translators wrote, "They are so romantic, like movies from the thirties." Her comment helped me to see the letters in a historical light, including the ideas of love and romance. Above all, the letters represented the perspectives of young people who were secular, urban Jews, leftist in their politics, not Zionist, well educated, and seeking a future for themselves in France. They typify a particular moment in Polish Jewish history when both middle class men and women alike took advantage of the possibility to study in other countries and become professionals. Virtually all of their friends were Jews, both in Poland and France, who studied at one of the universities in France. My father worked in a restaurant specifically for émigré Jewish students. Among his friends all were atheists, most or all identifying themselves as "leftists": two were fervent Communist Party members, at times on the run from the police, because of their politics. For the most part they came from middle class families who could afford to educate their children in private schools. Many of these families fell on hard times in the thirties, like my grandparents, and they could no longer support their children.

My father in Paris, circa 1930

The 1930s in Poland was a devastating decade. Poland suffered a deep and lasting depression and a political right wing resurgence. Jewish students were thrilled to be away from Poland. My mother refers to what is happening in Poland as "hell" in one of her letters. I assume she is referring to the depression that affected both my parents' families. As the letters reveal, neither could afford to help their children financially. She may also have been thinking of the rise of anti-Semitic incidents, which were beginning in the early thirties and became particularly virulent after my parents settled permanently in Paris.

Both of my parents were fluent in French. My mother already was before she studied in Grenoble, and by the time my father moved to Paris he was as well. Their politics, their ideas of friendship, romance, and marriage constituted a belief system that was unique to this moment for Jewish/Polish urban, secular, well educated young people attempting to create a life for themselves that was very different from their parents' lives. France above all offered freedoms that were no longer possible in Poland, including access to higher education in a country that welcomed foreign students.

**Friends and my father, second from right. Friends include Mark Zborowski
(first on left with beret) and Bolek Bejslechem (2nd/no beret)**

Despite similarities in my parents' views on love and commitment, they differed somewhat in their views of gender roles. My father was the more egalitarian. In his letters, he insists on my mother's completing her degree by taking her final exams in Business Law from the University of Grenoble. He strongly urged my mother to take this exam so she could find employment that paid a decent salary. My mother focused on their relationship and the extent to which she felt her love was returned. Often she felt uncertain of my father's love, especially at the beginning of their correspondence, and expressed her fear and disappointment in my father. Although she was always willing to spend every ounce of her energy earning money for the two of them, she did not share my father's desire to acquire a profession.

One of the many hotels in Paris where my father lived.

As a daughter, I recognized personality characteristics that were lifelong, such as my father's conscientiousness in studying and "improving" himself. He also had many friends to whom he was loyal throughout his life. He needed my mother, not only as lover and companion, but also to learn how to connect with people emotionally since his own mother was, in his words, a "hard" and judgmental person, but he was close to his kind, gentle father. My mother helped him become attuned to his feelings and to express them. She was his champion who adored him. But she also chastised him for his inability to convey his feelings and his focus on "facts" rather than emotions. His letters reveal changes in his emotional expressiveness, and he acknowledges this proudly: he feels like a different, more open, and more introspective person.

Much of my mother's life was dedicated to supporting my father in his career and creating a warm and welcoming home. My father's interests became hers, as she helped support him through medical school and during my childhood ran the office, acting as secretary, nurse, and manager. These aspects of my parents were already emerging in their early twenties.

The Love Story

The story began in the summer of 1930 when my mother returned to her home in Lodz after completing her first year at the University of Grenoble, a return seemingly necessitated by declining family finances as Poland's depression deepened. My father, who chose to stay and find work, found a room to rent. The landlady, Madame Jacquier, a lively, practical eighty-two-year-old woman, took an instant liking to him and immediately made him the object of her care and affection. In the letter below, my father jokes about her solicitous care but clearly basks in it.

The letter to my mother, his first one after her departure to Lodz via Vienna, describes his new landlady as well as his job for the summer:

Grenoble, July 3, 1930

My Sweetest,

I received both of your letters and I am happy that you had such a good time in Vienna.

As far as I am concerned a lot has changed. First I found a great first floor apartment in a villa, which boasts a marvelous garden. I am free to use it. Additionally, the apartment has a small sitting room — all of it costs 130 francs a month.[3] The lady of the house is wonderful and I think she still has some vacant apartments. If you'd like, you could also find a room with her.

As far as the landlady is concerned, she is 82, has a radio and "torments" me with her care. Quite accidentally I slipped and mentioned that I was once sick.[4] She grabbed onto that and decided that from now on I need to practice "sub alimentation." Because of that she is determined to cook me a horsemeat steak every night for free. She drops in with a glass of sweetened wine, and she brings milk, fruit preserves, etc. To top that she makes me breakfast before I go to the factory every day. It consists of half a liter of milk that is so fatty it makes me cringe. Additionally, I get two slices of bread with as much butter as I desire. For that I pay her 50 francs. In the evening I have to show her what I got for myself for supper. Next she complains that it isn't nourishing enough.

Now it is Saturday evening. I didn't work after dinner so I decided to take a bath. I shaved my head and I look like a prisoner sentenced to hard labor. Forgive me Hala that I list all the news randomly, without order. I really want to write you about everything so I put down everything that comes into my mind.

The last few days I have been a little sick. I have a feeling that it is the aftermath of my bike ride in the rain. From time to time, I have a stabbing pain in my back and I decided that I would use the cupping therapy.[5] I called for Jasza [a friend from Lodz] *to help me and he has just left. Actually, I feel better already. Just in case though I am going to get more cups at the pharmacy tomorrow and Jasza is going to apply them again. Apart from that, my landlady massages my back with iodine before I go to bed.*

My job at the factory is quite easy. I have already learned how to run the machinery for the bridge, and it is easy now. As a rule I am busy two or three hours a day. I am sitting and I just move the wheel one way or another. The remainder of my time I devote to reading. I only regret that I cannot write because I am covered with machine grease and oil.

Halus, my darling, I think that I already wrote you everything about myself. I kiss you very, very warmly and I bid you good-bye, Michal

P.S. Tell me how our visit with my old folks went and write about everything.

My parents' letters often crossed, and my father was not as frequent a correspondent as my mother. She wrote about missing him and her love, and he wrote about what he was doing. She began to despair of the relationship and my father's loyalty and love. My mother's next letter was written before she received my father's letter. She chastises him for not writing enough — a constant theme in her letters.

July 7, 1930

Dearest Mus,

You are very bad. I understand that you are quite busy and that you prefer anything else to writing letters but at the same time it doesn't mean that you should leave the two of my letters unanswered. I miss you so very much, but despite that I wouldn't have written except that I do not want to withhold the money. I know for sure you need it.

Mus, please don't think that I am angry. I am simply very sad. Especially that the situation at home it not good. I am not even talking about our less than booming business, but my mother's health is very bad. Doctors fear that she might have pernicious anemia.

As I mentioned, I visited your parents. They received me exceptionally well. They both made a very pleasant impression on me, especially your father. They kept me for two hours although I was in a great hurry because my parents were going to the theater that evening. I told them all about you and when your father heard that you were studying two things at once [chemistry and medicine] he was afraid that it might be too difficult for you. They also aren't thrilled about your job. They fear it is too hard. I was trying to convince them that the job is not tiring. Now I ended up with the following result: I convinced them somewhat but I am worried myself that you work too much. Musieniek, if you ever feel like writing me back, please tell me the truth about how you are and whether your job doesn't exhaust you too much.

I am writing again about your parents. We talked about money and your dad said that he would send you some cash not later than the ninth. Apart from that I let them know that the additional 100 francs a month[6] would wonderfully improve your income.

It is difficult to write about myself because I am a little bit afraid that I would write too much nonsense.

For the time being, I kiss you very, very much,
Yours, Hala

My father was not a consistent correspondent, and, when he wrote, it was mainly about friends, his job, and plans for the coming semester. My mother writes a despairing and disparaging letter which I quote in part:

August 13, 1930

My dearest Musienick,

Now I know that you absolutely don't love me at all. I got your letter yesterday and I couldn't answer right away because our house was full of people....

You write that you are busy in the evenings because you have to read books and you go to bed very early. I would gladly believe that, but if I wanted to write to you I am sure that I would be able to find a moment to write a few lines. Besides there is always something called an English Saturday with its long evening and there is Sunday. In other words I have an impression that the reason you don't write is not the shortage of time but the lack of desire. There is a Russian saying that "you cannot force love." I think you will understand it because the words are very similar to Polish. I decided Musieniek to make your task easier. Please don't think that I am writing it all as a complaint. I simply don't want you to feel that I am your obligation; not only now but even if we were married. You can be free at any moment. If writing letters seems to be a forced labor to you I wouldn't accept them under any circumstances. Anything would be more welcome!

I don't have the final page of this letter but by the next letter, my mother's tone changes dramatically. My father responds to her feelings in this way in his letter written the same day:

August 13, 1930

Halus,

I admit that you are right. The real truth is that I don't like to write letters and don't know how to. Before your departure you even admitted that you knew about it very well. You said that you wouldn't be mad at me and that you wouldn't demand to have your every letter answered. Halus, please tell me do you really feel so unhappy when you get my letters with a one or two day delay? If so, I solemnly swear that I will write to you regularly from now on.

My mother accepted my father's apologies and she continued to make plans for her return to Grenoble, which included bringing clothes that my father needed. She promised to arrive in mid-October and if the landlady has a vacancy she said she would take it. She notes, "*Please forward my regards to her because I can tell from your letters that she is an exceptionally pleasant woman.*"

One of the painful aspects of my mother's situation was that my father's mother, Roza Wolkowicz, whom he described as a difficult woman, clearly made my mother very uncomfortable. In August, she writes about an excruciating visit from her.

August 25, 1930

My dearest Musienick,

I got your letter and as usual I write you right away. I start with the issue that is most current now, that is with your mother... She stayed with us for three hours and I have to admit that I was so nervous that I couldn't focus that evening at all. I made an impression of a person who wasn't quite conscious.

And now apropos of that visit. I am not sure if I wrote to you that the first time your mother was here she got to know only my mother. The second time she got to know my father, Fredek and Pola.[7] This time the three of us stayed together for quite some time — that means both mothers and me. I felt like a person ready to be raked over burning coals. I wanted to run away, because like you, I had an impression that your mother has ideas about quite a few things. She was showering me with compliments and was asking my mother about everything. During the conversation she repeated quite a few times that you are 20.[8] I have to admit that it spoiled quite a few things for me, as I claimed the whole time that you are my [age] peer. Later during a tete a tete with my parents I managed to explain that it was what you told me to say; but it spoiled things for me. I have to admit that if there were more visits like this one, I would most likely end up in Tworki.[9]

I was so strangely sad and I had an impression that they were checking me out. Ach, Musieniek, it was unspeakably painful. You ask me what impression your mother made on me. It is hard for me to answer because I wasn't watching and observing unemotionally. I was extremely nervous.

My dearest Musieniek, I would so very much like for these two months to be over because honestly I am fed up with vacation. I must be very much in love since I want to finish my freedom so quickly. Fredek left two days ago and I am so sad without him. I was honest with him and I didn't need to pretend anything.

I didn't start to arrange my passport yet, because it doesn't take long nowadays, and I still have some time. I tried to influence my parents to let me leave earlier but I am not very pushy with that. I am sad to leave them here without me since I know they will miss me terribly. This year I learned how good they are for me, and that they accept my every whim. I kiss you very warmly,

Your Hala

It is clear that my mother had doubts about my father's love for her. His letters have disappointed her, and after his mother came to inspect her and questioned her age she felt humiliated. She was mortified that she had to lie and pretend that she is the same age as my father. The age difference didn't matter to her or to my father, but my father's mother, by his account, was a traditional and insensitive woman, and to her it mattered greatly. My mother has a resigned tone in this letter, sensing that she is leaving her parents for a love that may not be what she hoped.

Ultimately, she postponed her trip until the beginning of the semester in October. Clearly there was cooling off between my parents even as my mother continued her plans to return to Grenoble. The tone of the letters is friendly and business-like, focusing on arrangements and the possible position that my father was seeking in Grenoble where he would be apprenticed to a physician.

The next correspondence between my parents is between November 1931 and May 1932. By this time my father had moved to Paris, enrolled as a medical student, again balancing the need to make money and studying. She was eager to join my father in Paris, but he could not support her. My mother's parents also were not able to support her, even though by this time they had met my father and felt confident that he was a good person and right for their daughter. My mother was confronted with the need to earn enough money at least for the trip to Paris, and, she hoped, with some savings as well. She also would have had to return to Grenoble to take her final exams. My father insisted on this because it would enhance her prospects for employment.

Several of the letters reveal my father's engagement in leftist politics through his work in the restaurant run by the Foyer des Etudiants Juifs. The restaurant was sponsored by the association and frequented by foreign Jewish medical students. In these letters my father relates his struggles to keep himself afloat financially, at times indicating that he doesn't even have enough money to buy food. My mother is frantically trying to earn some money, keep her spirits up, and address her parents' worries about her leaving home for an unknown future and without means to support herself. She is also depressed and talks about seeing a physician who tells her that she needs "love"!

In the first letter from Paris, dated November 2, 1931, my father writes that he will be living with one of his closest friends, Szmajka, and "has a prepaid room" ready for his arrival. Although he moved several times, he always remained in the fifth arrondissement near the Sorbonne and the medical school. In this letter he describes his first apartment and his friends:

November 2, 1931

The room is on the second floor, it has warm and cold water and central heating––all that for 400 francs a month. We are in the best mood and we feel even better about our prospects for the future. We keep a tight group as if we were a family. That means besides myself and Szmajka, there is Gugber—an exceptionally nice boy. He has a great talent for physics. He already has his own patented invention. In our group are also Marek and Regina and Ber--he is a great guy in his fifth year of medical studies.[10] He lives with Gugber. In a month we will be starting our student restaurant. We have the money and everything else. In any case, you are part of the managementof the restaurant and your cooperation is ensured.

For now I bid you good-bye. I kiss you heartily and please stay optimistic. I promise that I love you and I didn't exaggerate anything in this card. I will give you details in my letters. Kiss your parents for me, send my regards to everyone, and thank them for seeing me ofi at the train station.

Michal

On November 6, 1931, my mother responds.

My Dearest Mus,

I got your card last evening. I didn't write right away because I had no paper. I have read it probably about twenty times over. It is so you! You fill me with so much hope and so much courage. And you know Musieniek, I lost my spirit completely after you had left. I couldn't think a single bright thought. After I read your card I cheered up. I realized that one way or another I would be with you soon.

You were writing about Ingber, Ber, Marek and Regina. Write a bit more about them. I'd like to know who your friends are. Musieniek, write me in detail about the restaurant. Where does the money come from, is it something realistic, can this plan be accomplished in the nearest future?

P.S. I am at grandma's place. My parents wanted to add a line but I will let them do it in my next letter. They ask me to kiss you warmly and to thank you for the card and your best wishes.

Kitty, please stay healthy, my darling, right?

The question mark sadly typifies my mother's fear when she is separated from my father that their relationship may not last. It is a fear that surfaces again and again, as does her acknowledgment of a depression that she tries hard to fight but cannot always overcome.

By this time, her parents had come to know my father and seem to have welcomed him as a future son-in-law.

My grandmother Mera writes to him shortly after his departure from Lodz:

Lodz, November 9, 1931

Our dearest Michalek,

Your letter arrived just about an hour ago and Halus had been waiting for it impatiently. She is eagerly writing her reply at this moment. I am sitting next to her and I decided to write a few lines of cordial greetings to you. We are so sad without you. We all miss you so very much at home. Our dinners are a sad affair, and Hala seldom joins us. I would so much want you to be together, and our Halus is very sad and she doesn't have any fun at all.

Tomorrow I will be receiving Artek [a much younger brother of my grandfather, closer in age to my mother] and his fiancée. It is so sad that you can't be together with us. This is all for now. I would like to write more but Hala wouldn't allow me to put off this letter any longer. I have to finish now. I kiss you and wish you success, health and good spirits.

Your always devoted,
Maria Rozin

Best regards from my husband. He is not at home at the moment.

It is clear that my grandparents embraced my father as a future son-in-law. I am moved by the love that my grandparents extended to my father, after getting to know him, and the way in which they drew him into the family. My father often told me that he felt very close to my mother's parents. My parents similarly welcomed my future husband when he began to see me frequently, and I am struck by the similarity in openness and warmth they showed toward him. Clearly my maternal grandparents set a precedent for both of my parents in embracing the person whom their child chose to love.

In my father's subsequent November 7, 1931, letter to my mother, he explains the proposed restaurant. Apparently, his friend Szmajka befriended a businessman from Austria interested in a business venture of a student cafeteria in Paris. He has promised to finance the venture himself. According to my father, the restaurant is *"supposed to be a source of income for Marek and Regina, and for Ingber and Ber. Prior to December I will remain poor, of course."* When my father notes that Marek is not getting any money from the Party, he is being circumspect here. Clearly he is aware of Marek's political work, but I am certain he does not know the details. Marek became a Communist as a teenager and remained active in the Party. The other friends whom he mentions I never met or heard about. He continues in this letter:

I told Szmajka what a great cook you are and that you could make salads and cookies that my mom was enraptured about. Our restaurant could send you money in December so that you could join us.[11]

Sweet Halus, you have no idea how much pleasure writing this letter brings me. I have never enjoyed writing letters in my life and now I do, for the first time.

As far as being in this "commune," to which I automatically belong, the matter stands as follows: whoever has the means covers the bills. Upon my arrival I had the money and I was the one paying for the first few days, as long as I could. Naturally I set aside money to sign up for the university classes and to cover other necessary expenses. Of course the money ran out really quickly and now we are waiting for new cash.

As far as medicine is concerned, my papers were ready and I have signed up. I have already worked in the hospital for two days. I am going to lectures, but I don't have any books. It is a serious hindrance.

Dear Halus, can you believe that I can't stop writing this letter. It is unbelievable. I could never sit and write without getting up and pausing. I am writing this letter swiftly, without stopping, as if I were afraid I would forget something if I stopped. I write a letter like this for the first time in my life.

Halus, can you believe me? I miss your parents so much. I like being with them a lot and I would like to see them again. Send my regards to all. Thank all who have seen me ofi. Kiss your mother and father and tell them that I love them as much as my own father [it is notable that my father only mentions his father, and not his mother]. *Ask them to write me.*

Halus I can't stop writing but I have to finish. Write about everything. I hug you once again and kiss you first on your lips, then on your forehead, and then playfully on your nose. Szmajka is sending you his regards too — I don't want to wake him up because he has just fallen asleep.

Bye darling,
Michal

My father followed up with a letter on November 28, 1931, in which he again vows his love for my mother and excitedly talks about work prospects including tutoring Polish students in French as well as the promised restaurant job, for which he needed a recommendation from a rabbi. Clearly my father had connected with Polish/Jewish students in Paris and was able to use these connections to find work in order to sustain himself. At the same time he notes that he is studying hard for his "bones" exam that, if passed, will allow him to begin classes in dissection. He also notes that if all these plans come together he will be earning 600 francs a month (approximately $24 dollars) and can easily bring my mother to Paris.

My mother responds to this letter on December 2, 1931, in which she describes her financial situation as grim. She has been unable to find work, and it is clear that her parents cannot support her return to Paris. She writes *"my budget equals zero. I am really trying. I am looking for students or a job but unfortunately without results."* She attributes this to the bad times in Poland and that "ladies cannot afford the luxury of French lessons."

My father told me several times that he did not have enough money to eat in the early days in Paris. His parents were not able to send him money, and his job opportunities in the beginning were not sufficient to support his room and board. In a letter that crossed my mother's letter of December 2, 1931, my father writes that he has had not been responding to my mother's letters because he is literally starving.

December 2, 1931

Halus you don't know what happened to me. At that time [he is referring to time when he didn't respond to my mother's letters] *I almost died of hunger in Paris. Halus this is the truth. Now I can write what was hidden between the lines before. I can write about it because it isn't true any more. I was starving for two weeks. Halus, you don't know what it means to be laying prostate on the bed without having anything to eat. In such a state, when I could hardly move my legs or feet, I had to go to a lecture. I was falling asleep from emaciation and exhaustion.*

Halus, you don't know that feeling when you are lying on a bed in the evening and you can't fall asleep because of hunger. You feel like these are your last hours and you don't have strength enough to even make yourself eat. I gladly survived because I knew that you would be proud of me one day when I would tell you about it.

Halus I can write about it now because it is all history. I was bothering the president [he means of the Foyer des Etudiants Juifs] *and Brzezinski and I wouldn't leave the restaurant. They knew I was starving and that they couldn't get rid of me. I was dying of starvation to the point that I could even eat a plate itself so they finally gave me the job.*

So that issue became a thing of the past — that means the food. Now for the second issue. I have French classes now [meaning he is tutoring Polish students in French]. *The pay is not too good, only 6 francs an hour, but the work is easy.*

Sweet Halus, it is already half past one. I am going to bed because I have a lecture early in the morning in the hospital. I will write to you tomorrow again and now I will be still thinking about you for a long time tonight.

Good night Halutka, sleep well.
I kiss you, Michal

On December 9, 1931, Halina responds compassionately to this letter and asks Mikhal's forgiveness for her lack of understanding of his situation:

My Darling Mus,

I received your letter this morning, although it got to Lodz last night. It was a holiday and they weren't delivering letters. Musinek, you wrote that it was your fourth letter. That means that one was lost. I hope that we will be able to avoid any more nuisances like that. You know darling, after I read your letter, it seemed to me that I was the worst person in the universe.

You were starving and I didn't even think about it, nor did I help you. I can't even cry when I think about it. I am so distraught and so sad that I can't even express it with words. None of my letters, and this one in the least, can express my thoughts. My dearest sunshine,

I fully appreciate your love. I can't fully express what it means to me. It fills my heart with pride and happiness.

It is true that I never went hungry, but I would agree to anything to be with you. Unfortunately, I can't tell that to anyone, and I am afraid that you wouldn't take it at face value. You probably think I am a girl who doesn't know real life, a girl who thinks she would be able to shoulder everything, whereas in reality, she would be able to withstand nothing.

If you could spend one night with me and see how much I miss you, how I cannot find interest in anything, then you would wish me anything but the loneliness I have to endure now. I don't know why I wrote all that [referring to her previous letter in which she doubted Mikhal's love since she had not received answers to her letters]. *I know that you want to be with me. I had to say out loud my everyday thoughts which I cannot tell to anyone.*

You see my darling, my departure doesn't look very good. At the moment I am not making any money and everything fails me. Everybody is complaining that times are bad and that they cannot afford the luxury of French lessons. You can understand how I get upset with all that. I feel that if I stay here alone, I will go crazy. I miss you day and night.

Musienik, please write what you think about my departure. Will I have to miss you much longer. A propos of what you written, that you were hungry and weak, and instead of running around town with Szmajka, you were going to classes for me – Muszka, I can't thank you enough. But if I can make you happy with my love, you are going to be the happiest person on earth. Muska, I love you endlessly and madly.

Darling, I don't want to forget: this month on Tuesday, Artek is getting married. Please send him your congratulations – for me. Put the letter inside a letter to me. But don't be late because I will encounter much unpleasantness. Besides, I think I will need Artek's help.

My sweet darling, I think that I wrote about everything. I kiss you very warmly, your madly in love, Hala.

Kind regards from my parents and uncle and aunt Polakov

I recognize my mother in these love letters – certainly her deep and abiding love and passion for my father, but also the feeling of falling into an abyss when everything was not falling into place.

My father replies on December 13, 1931. The key sentences in this letters are:

December 13, 1931

Please try to get your passport ready and study hard for your exam. You have no idea how important it is. In summer I will have an extra 800 francs a month in addition to my daily allowance. It would be great if you had a diploma and were able to earn some money too. Therefore, if you love me and if you want us to be together, we really shouldn't make any more mistakes. You should work hard to get your diploma.

In his letter of January 10, 1932, my father tells my mother about the restaurant where he is working as a waiter and the political conflicts that may undermine its existence. It is clear that despite his seemingly apolitical stance he is supportive of the position taken by the organization he describes: Kampf [in German, struggle], a leftwing political group.

January 10, 1932

Halinka my sweetest!

Halus I have so much to tell you. First of all, I spent my New Year's Eve at a ball given by Combat — in Yiddish Kampf. It is one of the sub-sections of the U.F.E.[12] This organization is strong in Paris and it is tied to the Foyer des Etudiants Juifs. Naturally, the "ball" wasn't just a dance afiair. They had a program, recitations and a skit about the management which was quite good.

Finally I want to tell you that my waiter's job is in jeopardy. Essentially I am not a Kampf man, or at least I am not an active member. I gave my word to Brzezinski [the manager] that as a waiter in the cafeteria I would be neutral. I am keeping my word and everyone likes the job I do here. But the Kampf people feel strongly and they come here in great numbers for dinner. They have mass meetings and hand out fliers. (A propos, let's keep it between us, but objectively speaking they are right. Although they [Assocation des Etudiants Juifs] are philanthropists, their dinners are not good, but expensive. They act as usurpers and G and other management have fat salaries).

To put it briefly there are fights at dinner time almost every day. There is more bloodshed every day and with time the management and the manager asked for the police to come. They were throwing people out and arresting some. The restaurant is now constantly stafied with police. Despite this they [Kampf] are strong in numbers. Additionally, this is Paris and not Grenoble. Since they stay in contact with Jewish and other nations' labor unions, they have [supporters] at their disposal. At their command, the men can demolish a place and level it to the ground. That's why there are rumors that if they don't stop what they are doing, the restaurant will be closed and the Association will be disbanded. Of course the waiters and the entire stafi stay neutral and don't participate.

Halinka, at this moment I think I have a strong feeling that you are upset with me. Halus, I cannot express to you everything that I am feeling now. Sometimes it comes easier to me than today. But if you knew how much I miss you, how much I think about you, how I even talk to strangers about you. I know I will never be able to convince you about the sincerity of my feelings towards you. You always had and will have a shadow of doubt.

Halus, please write back to me. Prove that I am wrong, tell me how things are with work and money. Would you for sure be able to come in

June? Halus, how is your mother, is she better? Please send my deepest regards to your parents.

Same to Grandma Polakov and everybody else.

Halus, I kiss you unceasingly,
Michal

On January 18, 1932, my father writes again about the restaurant. He notes that he, who felt that he was not a "political person," is now representing the waiters to the management.

As far as I am concerned, things are not too bad. They are not in a hurry to close the restaurant because business is too good, and I am a very good worker. I also have too many connections for them to fire me [I believe he is referring to his friends who originally helped to organize this restaurant]. *Additionally I have to tell you that I represent all the waiters and one of their three board members. As such I organize and run the waiters' movement and I represent them outside. So far everything got quieter here. Our management caved in and they started to negotiate with Kampf. They* [management] *allowed the distribution of fliers since apparently the police threatened to disband the Association if the situation continues.*

Folks at home must be doing pretty badly with money now because they can't even send me 100 zloty.[13] Just recently I got a letter from home that they will send me some money. Right now I live like a beggar. If it weren't for my studies, which I cannot neglect, of course, I could find all sorts of jobs here in Paris and I could live quite well. You can find a job here if you want to, but I cannot forget about my ultimate goal and therefore I cannot devote too much time to that. Halus you cannot imagine how happy I will be when you pass your exam. I care about it tremendously!

Halus, please write to the university for a certificate that you need to take your exam. I have a feeling that even your father is not opposing this trip. He wants you to get a diploma. My sweet Halus, I have a pretty room, although it is on the fourth floor. It has central heating and hot and cold water. It overlooks Notre Dame and the rivers.

For now I kiss and hug you very tightly. Please write back to me right away. Send my regards to everyone, and please send me the Luster's powder,[14] my sweetie.

Mus

My father is loving but consistent in urging my mother to take her exams and complete her degree.

On January 26, 1932, my father writes further about the political situation in the restaurant and that he has become an activist "against his will":

> *I have neglected my studies recently and against my will become an activist. As you know though, this sort of work doesn't lie in my character. There is too much "buzz" with this and a person can't even find a moment to focus and study. After the recent troubles with the police here in the dining hall, we had a drop in customers. You had to hear about it and your dad could read about it in Hajut* [a Yiddish newspaper published in Warsaw]. *Because of that the management from the Foyer des Etudiants Juifs offered that we could choose five waiters whom we wanted fired. That was supposed to help the budget.*
>
> *Naturally, we summoned all the waiters to a meeting and we unanimously agreed that we wouldn't fire anyone. Should someone get fired, we would all go on strike. We immediately contacted Kampf and they were supposed to come to the restaurant and help form a strike fighters group. We were printing fliers the whole night. The fliers were directed to our customers and they were asking them to support us.*
>
> *Our plan was as follows… the director comes and asks if we chose the five to go. At that point, I would tell her that we all join the waiters in solidarity. If she chooses to fire the five waiters, we would all quit. Then we would pass out our fliers to all the customers. I and another committee member would talk with all present and ask them to unite with us so that the five others wouldn't be fired.*
>
> *But it never came to that though. The Director asked if we chose five. We went to see her all together and I told her what I just described. She said that she would forward the message to the Foyer des Etudiants Juifs and the second part of our plan did not happen. Instead, all the students had a discussion about the recent events and asked all the students to unite in case there would be a strike. This resolution was passed unanimously. That's why the management and its leader, G, couldn't oppose it. Our action became lawful in this way. In short, after such a course of events the Foyer had no other course but to surrender entirely.*
>
> *If you really want to know what happened there at the dining hall I advise you to get a Warsaw newspaper, Nasz Przglad from January 22. It has an article, I am afraid a stupid one, entitled "Waiters from Latran Street."*[15]

In this letter my father again emphasizes the importance of my mother taking her exams and passing:

> *My thoughts are that when you come to France at the beginning of May, you need to go straight to Paris. I think that staying here till June wouldn't cost you too much. You'd be here one week before the exam. Then you'd go to Grenoble for two weeks because that is how long the exams would take. We'll find the money for that. In any case I firmly insist you should pass your exams before vacation starts. And now I will explain why. It is impossible to get a summer job in Paris without a certificate of diploma. It is quite different and possible when you have one.*
>
> *In any case, your diploma is invaluable. That's why I care so much that you pass, and that you pass with flying colors. In summer you will be able to look for a permanent job and this job will decide everything for us. Then we would certainly be able to survive the next year here in Paris.*

My father assumes the role of mentor and advisor in this letter to my mother. I understand his position. He needs to finish one more year of courses to earn his degree. Until then he needs my mother to hold a job, and he is convinced that if she gets her diploma from Grenoble after taking her final exam, she would be able to find a job easily.

In his letter of February 3, 1932, my father complains of how hard and exhausting waiting tables is. He then goes on to describe his daily schedule:

> *10 a.m. to 12 noon I am at the hospital and right afterwards I go to the restaurant. I stay there until 1:30, and then I literally run to the dissecting room, where I work from 1:30 to 3:30. I don't know if you realize what a dissecting room work entails. The room is stuffy and you need to constantly make very precise incisions. It is very tiring to start with and even more so if you already come there tired. And now I go twice a week to give a French class after the dissecting room. Since the class isn't a regular class, I get 5 francs each time. All together it brings me 30 francs a month which is pretty much nothing.*

My father also notes in this letter that he has a job prospect and if he got it he would be "totally happy." He also writes that his father has written to him that he is not in a position to send him money until the end of the month. My grandfather Aron wrote of himself: *You see, this is a picture of a man who has no money.*

My father feels very badly about asking his father for money and writes to my mother: *If I could I would have sent the money back to my father.*

The job my father is pursuing comes through while writing these letters. It is to be a personal secretary to a physician whose specialty is "venereal disease, lungs and rheumatism."

On February 10, 1932, my father describes the job he has applied for: *I have learned that this old nutty doctor, a maniac, a perfectionist and a curmudgeon is accepting medical students to his practice.*

This is my father's description of the job which would pay him 300 francs a month plus room and board:

> *This is how I would work: at 7:45 in the morning I need to be in his bedroom. I do a hand massage on him (I learn how to do this), then I pick up the mail. I look at the prospects, and give him a summary. This lasts until 9:30. At 9:30 I go to the hospital* [owned by this physician] *and I stay there until 12. At the moment I am not sure of my work so afterwards I go and work as a waiter. If I stay at the clinic instead then I would go to dinner and next go to the dissecting room. After the dissecting room at 4 p.m. I return to the clinic where I work either with the doctor or I go downstairs to the pharmacy and I stay there until 8 in the evening. From 8 to 12 in the evening I study. I am sure that you understand that for us it is a huge step forward. And now Halus I am sure that you understand that it will be enough that you have a diploma and I guarantee you a job in Paris. We would then rent a quite nice apartment and let our parents know when we go to the ofiicials* [he means to get married]. *This is what I have been fighting for since the beginning of the year and that's why I put such an emphasis on your diploma and on studying. I think that this* [his job] *is a career starter for me.*

In this letter he also describes his current work in medical school:

> *Halus, you ask how I am doing in the hospital and the dissecting room. The dissecting room bores and tires me. I think this is the worst year of all because of anatomy. I am not as good as it as you think. You know how easy it is to distract me from working and I need perfect conditions. The hospital is another matter — working there is very interesting…. At the moment I am working in the surgery department and I am not very interested in surgery. Starting in March I will be working in the internal medicine department. It is the department that interests me the most.*

I am again struck by my father's vision for my mother and their future which he sees as dependent on her getting her diploma. He felt that they should both earn a degree and that would facilitate my mother's getting a good job.

What strikes me is my father's boundless energy to seek out new opportunities, to try things, and to be honest with my mother and himself about what interests him and doesn't and about his work habits. I also recognize his need for absolute quiet and calm in order to study because he was easily distracted. As the physician I knew he was extraordinarily disciplined about keeping up in his field, reading journals, and taking courses; he also required total quiet so that he could concentrate.

In the February 19, 1932, letter he reports that the job didn't pan out. After a few days of work, he realizes that "I wouldn't be able to study at all. I was coming home at 8:30 and it was obvious to me I wouldn't be able to learn well enough to be on the right level." But he retains his optimism:

Somewhere in Paris lives a little boy who constantly thinks how to make his little girl happy in this world. He is sure that he will do well in this life and that they will be doing well and that he loves her (her name is Halineczka) to distraction. In any case, I drew a conclusion that I won't go under here in Paris. Hunger is for me a thing from the past. Here in Paris I made some sort of a name for myself.

Halus, my sweetest darling, I love you more every day. The closer it comes to your arrival, the more convinced I am that we are going to do fabulously here together. I can't wait for this year to finish because quite frankly it has been nasty. First of all, because you are not here and secondly because the first year medical studies requires daily dissecting room classes. They take a lot of time and in addition I have plenty to do and to study. It is not the case in the second year or third year in medicine. Both of them are much easier, and I will have plenty of free time. That's why next year, I will do "physique generale" in order to get a "Licence d'Etat"/a state license. This is going to make things easier for us. Halus, you cannot imagine how I am looking forward to that moment when we will not depend on people any more. I see this picture with my eyes and treasure it. And you know, it is also possible that when you get a good job and I will also have one, then we will rent a room in Paris and we will go the mayor and we will send our parents wedding notices.

In a March 5, 1932, letter my father alludes to the difficult situation that his friend, Marek Zborowski, was in. It is clear that my father both supports Marek's politics and is in close touch with him. According to recent research he was a spy for the NKVD (the equivalent of the CIA in the Soviet Union) probably throughout his days in Paris and briefly in the United States.[16] He was assigned to befriend Trotsky's son, Lev Sedov, then living in Paris, and became his secretary and friend.

> *The police have started to pay attention to Marek and the two of them* [he is referring to Marek's wife Regina] *had to separate. They went deep into debt beforehand. The amount was 1200 francs. Marek left Grenoble and Regina is in Lodz at the moment. They are supposed to meet in Germany in two months and then leave for Russia. If you want you can visit Regina or ask her to come over to your place. I think you would enjoy talking to her.*

Mark, Regina, and my parents remained friends throughout their student days and in the United States, including when Mark was imprisoned in 1962 in the federal prison in Danbury, Connecticut, for his Communist Party activities in the United States, which he always denied.

For her birthday my father shares a lovely thought that his good friend Szmajka shared with him, "Szmajka has a vision of dancers for a life time, and he thinks we are one of them. He thinks I am a 'dancer' and you are an ideal partner."

My father sends my mother a book for her birthday, writing on April 20, 1932:

> *I thought it would be right for you to have this book since we are just about to start "dancing" our dance of life together. Besides this Halus you should know that on the 22ⁿᵈ* [my mother's birthday], *which is the day you are going to be reading this letter, I will be dressed "festively" and I will be in a happy mood. I will smile at the world and I will celebrate. You are going to hurt my feelings tremendously should you not do the same.*

My mother faced difficult decisions because she did not earn enough money to travel to Paris, and her parents tried to dissuade her from joining my father in Paris. She writes:

March 17, 1932

Darling, the real torture at home starts now. I argued with my mother, and with my father things aren't well either. Can you imagine! They don't want me to leave. They think that I am childish. My mother tells me it wouldn't be too terrible if I didn't get to see you for a couple of years. She is so egotistic that she doesn't want to sacrifice her views on proprieties even for my good. She can clearly see that I sufier and that I miss you. She considers my entire trip "inappropriate." You understand that I won't take it into consideration. I only wait to get enough cash and I will go!

I can only imagine the turmoil and pain my mother felt at this time. She has no money to speak of from her tutoring and piano lessons. Her parents are against her going to Paris, and my father's mother also does not support their relationship. This is the first time, my mother speaks about her parents' concern with "proprieties." I assume that my parents lived together once my mother arrived in Paris. She once told me that she had an illegal abortion in Paris, most likely before she and my father married. She told me that it was frightening, but as always, even in the telling, she spoke of it as something she could manage.

I sense from her letters to my father at this point that she is near a breakdown.

April 14, 1932,

My mother drags me through hell because I am leaving. Even at night I have terrible nightmares, my nerves are completely wrought and I cannot control myself. And I need my energy especially now. I am leaving against my parents' will. I will go because I think I should. The life I have now cannot be called life. It's vegetation and I don't want to vegetate as any cost. There is no pleasure in my life, nothing but constant arguments, misery and trouble. When I think that for so long I've been trying to get out of this hell hole, I lose heart.

Clearly, my mother was in a depression, tormented by what she felt was an empty life in Lodz, her parents' insistence that she not leave, and her desire to create a new life for herself with my father. She must also have felt that doing so was frightening and risky. Could she make a living? Would their love withstand the difficulties they faced? All this must have been overwhelming and depressing.

April 30, 1932

I have been studying a lot and still do. I am almost crazy with anxiety, but I think I will be able to pass now. I am only concerned about another issue, that the trip and my stay in Grenoble is going to undermine my finances.

> *I also fear that we are not going to have enough money to even find a job. I think that we will solve this problem in Paris.*

Her last sentence is telling. Whatever the difficulties, she believes that she and my father will sort them out. And they did. Finally she left Lodz at the end of May 1932 and joined my father for the rest of their lives. My mother never took her final exams in Grenoble.

This moment in her life was a decisive one. Since she never took her exams she did not have a degree from the University of Grenoble.[17] My mother instead chose to be with my father and not complete her degree. This was a choice that influenced the rest of her life.

Being a student was something that never interested her. But beyond this, I believe that the role division that developed during my parents' early days in Paris my mother supporting my father's career in a variety of ways persisted throughout their lives. Perhaps she never felt the desire to pursue her own dreams, or perhaps her dream was always to be part of a loving couple. She may have been afraid of failing her exam.

I know that as soon as she arrived in Paris, she began to work to support my father and herself. She took any job that she could find: tutoring, cleaning apartments, sewing. Eventually, she became expert at making French leather gloves, which she sold to fashionable stores and individuals. She also did embroidery for trousseaus and tutored Polish students in French. Somehow my parents survived through these odd jobs until my father received his medical degree and began to earn a living.

My father completed medical school and earned the MD degree in his field, ophthalmology. He fell in love with medicine. This is something that he told me over and over that he loved what he did. It was an important message to me. And I could see and feel his passion even when I was a child. He liked caring for his patients. Over dinner, he talked about the people he especially liked; he was proud of his diagnoses of difficult cases; he especially enjoyed treating children and was adept at making them feel comfortable; and he conscientiously kept abreast of his field.

When he chose ophthalmology as his field of specialization, his supervisor and mentor was a woman who came from a long, distinguished line of physicians dating back to the Court of Louis XVI, Docteur Delthil. Having an accomplished woman physician as a mentor made a tremendous difference in my father's life. It turned him into a feminist and an advocate for women in medicine. In the U.S., his supervisor was also a woman when he had to redo his internship, and they became friends. When I was fifteen and traveled with my parents to Paris, my father took me to meet Dr. Delthil. We went to a grand apartment in the 15th arrondissement where Dr. Delthil presided over tea. I could see that she delighted in my father's professional success.

These letters capture something that I knew about and recognized in my parents—a love that lasted throughout their lives. They also capture my father's boundless energy and enthusiasm for learning. As he got older he tried to develop many interests in addition to leading an incredibly busy life as a father, husband, physician, and researcher. He loved art and became an avid collector of paintings. He played tennis regularly, not very well but as in everything, he did his best. And most touching and important to me, he was a very good friend, as his letters demonstrate. He continued throughout his life to stay in touch with childhood friends, and, for those who survived the war, with his Paris friends.

My father was never politically active after his student days. It was too dangerous. He was warned by one of his professors in medical school that if he persisted in any leftist politics he would not be able to complete his studies. Clearly, someone was informing on my father. He made his choice then and never turned back.

Although he remained leftist in his political views throughout his life, he was careful not to share his political opinions outside our home. Throughout his years in practice, his office was located in a working class Polish Catholic neighborhood where he was beloved. Every Christmas we received abundant gifts from the many nuns whom he treated without charge. I still have embroidered tablecloths that they made for my parents.

At home my father taught me to be a critical thinker and to question what I read in newspapers. In the fifties, during the McCarthy hearings he had to be especially careful. In the hospitals where he worked (he was associated with three) he had to swear a "loyalty oath." He was especially careful with his colleagues not to discuss politics or reveal his own.

In the second half of the fifties he became alarmed because his lifelong friend Mark was charged with being a Soviet spy and was eventually tried and found guilty of perjury concerning his role in the Communist Party in the United States. He was imprisoned in Danbury, Connecticut's federal prison in 1962 with a four-year sentence but released for "good behavior" after two. My father insisted that Mark not call the house phone during the trial. He was afraid that our phone would be tapped. This may have been true. Mark and he had a falling out over this, which was eventually resolved when Mark was released from prison.

They remained friends, although more distant than before the trial. Mark and his wife, Regina, moved to San Francisco where Mark continued to have a successful career as an anthropologist. A friend of Margaret Mead and Ruth Benedict, he coauthored with Elizabeth Herzog *Life is with People: the Culture of the Shtetl* (1952), one of the most important books written in English at this time on the Jewish shtetl. My parents spent a summer with Mark and Regina in 1949 while he was working on the book. As staff anthropologist at Mount Zion Hospital and Medical Center, he wrote *People in Pain* (1969), in which he describes a study of attitudes of different ethnic groups to pain.

I was often annoyed as a teenager at what I thought was my father's overly cautious attitude about revealing his politics. Now I know that I was naïve. In the mid-fifties, during the McCarthy hearings and afterwards, it would have been very dangerous for him to speak his mind in any of his professional, or even friendship, circles. In the light of his caution, it was exciting for me to learn about his activism as a young man, even as he vowed that he was not an "activist," and about the strong stand and leadership he demonstrated in the successful negotiations with the management in the student restaurant on Rue Latran.

Although my father alluded to these moments in his life, knowing about them in detail, and the pride he took in his role, is important to me, as was his determination to succeed in medicine and to bring my mother to Paris in order for them to make a life together. I believe that Szmajka's image of the "dance" of life was a metaphor that my father took to heart. In many respects my parents negotiated this dance well, and with a great deal of pleasure and love for most of their lives. They were also literally good dancers. I still have my parents' Polish tango records and photos of them dancing.

If they could have chosen, my parents would have stayed in Paris their entire lives. However, in 1938 they received an amazing offer. My mother's grand uncle, Julius Love, a physician who lived in Philadelphia, visited my parents in Paris. A politically savvy man, he could see the writing on the wall regarding Nazism and the dangerous, widespread anti-Semitism in Germany. During his visit with my parents, he proposed that they emigrate to the States where he had a medical practice that he would turn over to them.

This was an offer hard to refuse. My parents were certainly aware that things were getting difficult in France following the fall of the Blum government in 1936 and the installation of a rightwing government. At home in Lodz, the depression was devastating for both families, and it was felt they could benefit from the income my parents would eventually earn in the U.S. My grandparents on both sides also believed they would be able to emigrate themselves after my parents established their practice and could provide affidavits. They all felt this was an opportunity that could not be refused. All of this seemed to make sense even though for my young parents, leaving Paris and their families was very difficult.

Uncle Julius Love and his wife Ida Love in Philadelphia circa 1938

In January 1938, Uncle Love wrote to my parents that they must hurry and obtain visas for otherwise the window for emigration would close.

Philadelphia, January 12, 1938[18]

Dear Galina and Michal!

Today we received your letter from January 2nd. We are very happy that you are getting your visa. It's a pity that you are in the situation, when you have to use it immediately. In my opinion, it's a result of some overlooking on the part of Mikhal: he should have organized things in a way that he would wait for visa, not visa for him.

In any case, I advise you to hurry with the arrival here because in today's circumstances and the situation in Europe, it's impossible [to know] what might happen. Sudden war, or a new project in congress can put an end to all hopes, and stop the Immigration here. And that's why I advise you to make haste with your interview.[19] As to what you should bring with you, I can tell you to bring everything you have[20] in terms of bedding, pillows, undergarments, and so on. It's not necessary to take medicine. Let Miachal take all the medical instruments that he can take. I advise him to take all kinds of linen towels that he uses. Once again, I am advising you to hurry with your arrival, and I am wishing you all the best.

Yours,
Julius Love

Give our regards to everybody when you will be in Poland. Write.
What's going on with this young man we met at your place in Paris? Where is he now? Did he go to (illegible). If he did go, tell him to write to me?[21]

My parents in their finest clothes shortly before leaving for the U.S.
(in front of Notre Dame)

At the time there was very little opportunity for Poles to emigrate except under the circumstances that Uncle Love proposed. He was a wealthy man; on the affidavit he signed to bring my parents to the States, he indicated that his assets were the equivalent of what today would be a million dollars.

My parents bid goodbye to their family and friends with the firm conviction that they would bring their parents to the States as soon as they could. They sailed on April 14, 1938, on the Isle de France and moved into Uncle Love's house at 315 Pine Street in Philadelphia.

But they never brought their parents to the States. My grandfather Sasha died in December 1938, and my grief- stricken grandmother wrote that she could not leave his gravesite. By the time she began to understand that she had no life in Poland anymore, it was too late to emigrate. If there had been a window of opportunity, it had closed. After the war in Europe was declared following the Nazis' invasion of Poland in September 1939, relatives begged my parents to bring them to the States. But this would not have been possible under the circumstances of the Nazi occupation: Jews were quickly labeled, stigmatized, ousted from their homes, and by 1940 restricted to ghettos.

My mother on the deck of the Isle de France, April, 1938

I believe that the burden of guilt for the loss of the entire families save for two survivors, Dosia and Adek, my father's cousins, whom my parents brought to the States after the war, marked my parents' lives irretrievably. When the loss is so great, there is no moment for grief. Losing everyone is beyond grief. For my parents it was unspeakable. In our family there were no conversations about the losses—only positive stories about my parents' growing up, about their parents and other relatives, and about their lives in Grenoble and Paris. The stories my parents told me helped me understand the love letters that I have quoted in this chapter. They looked back nostalgically at their early love, close friendships, and, for my father, learning a profession that defined his life.

My father's letter to my mother in 1932 from Paris

My mother's letter to my father in Paris from Lodz, 1932

Passport photos of my parents before leaving for U.S. in 1938

My mother dancing with her Uncle Artek. My father on right playing a flute, standing
my mother's cousin Adek on the mandolin, Bolek in center on the accordion.

Parents and family in Kolumna circa 1934. Standing left to right: father, mother, Bolek, Dora (maternal aunt), Adek (son of Dora). Seated: my grandmother Mera, Dora's husband, Artek.

My parents dancing circa 1937

My father rowing. Left: Guta Gurwicz, his cousin. Right: my mother.

Endnotes

1 Because this was a religious marriage, not a civil one, they had to have an official marriage and thus "remarried" in France during a summer vacation in 1936. This constituted their "legal" marriage certificate for all purposes going forward, including obtaining visas to the U.S. and passports.

2 The Association of Jewish Students, a philanthropic organization in France founded to help Jewish émigrés.

3 Approximately $5.

4 My father still was dealing with TB that he had contracted as an adolescent.

5 Cupping therapy is a form of alternative medicine in which cups are placed on the skin to create suction. The theory is that the suction of the cups mobilizes blood flow to promote healing.

6 $4.00 in 1930.

7 Fredek was my grandfather's youngest brother, six years older than my mother, and Pola was his wife.

8 My mother was two years older than my father.

9 A well-known Polish psychiatric hospital.

10 Of the students who are mentioned, I only know of Smajka Guriewicz, who eventually married a close friend of my father's, Guta, and Marek Zborowski (Mark in English), a close friend from high school. Regina L. (I do not know her maiden name) and he were not married yet but were comrades and a couple.

11 It is clear from the next letters that the restaurant never happened and my father was forced to take on waiting jobs on his own.

12 I have not found out what the initials stand for, but clearly it was a leftist student organization.

13 In 1930, 100 zloty equal approximately $27.

14 This was a powder that my father used as shampoo which he asked my mother to send regularly. My father, always well dressed, cared a great deal about his appearance.

15 The article was a satirical piece written to make fun of Jewish medical students who organize instead of studying. The newspaper, Nasz Przglad, was the best known, secular Jewish newspaper in Poland. The article was also published in the Yiddish newspaper Hajut.

16 Fox, "Mark Zborowski, the spy who came out of the Shtetl." Also, Zipperstein, "Underground Man: The Curious Case of Mark Zborowski and the Writing of a Modern Jewish Classic."

17 I have a Certificate from Grenoble indicating that she completed her course of study in French in 1929.

18 The letter is written in Russian, which my mother knew. Julius Love lived in Poland at a time when it was still incorporated into the Russian Empire.

19 Most likely, Uncle Love is talking about an interview with the Consul General which those trying to get visas had to go through.

20 Underlined in the original.

21 He may be referring to Mark Zborowski.

Chapter 3

Letters from Home, 1938–1941

Hope and Despair — Emigrating to
the United States, April 1938

My parents sailed for New York City aboard the Isle de France on April 14, 1938. Two weeks later, they were relieved to arrive in a place of safety at a moment when Jews were trying to flee Europe. They felt confident that in time they would bring their parents to the States. But they also felt great sadness in leaving their world behind. France was the place where they fell in love, where my father became a physician, and where they lived together for eight years. They had spent a third of their lives there.

My parents arrive in the U.S. April 1938. Date of photo, Sept. 8, 1938. From left: My mother's maternal uncle, Jack Kanne (changed from Jacob Kagan), my mother and father (smoking a cigar)

Given the quotas for Eastern Europeans established by the National Origins Immigration Act of 1924, there was little likelihood of their being granted a visa. The Act, which was in effect until 1965, aimed to "preserve the ideal of American homogeneity." It severely limited immigration from Eastern Europe and most of Asia, or even outlawed the immigration of those classified as "aliens," the Chinese and Japanese. For those allowed entry, visas were issued based on two percent of each national origin group in the U.S. at the base year of 1890. But far fewer were generally allowed in.

In most cases consuls would accept only the most probable guarantees of financial support, and they actually admitted fewer immigrants than were allowed in under the law. In the period of 1931-40 when my parents immigrated, fewer were allowed to emigrate from Eastern Europe than in the previous nine years. My parents had to convince the American consul in Poland that they would not become a "public charge" in the United States. It was clear from the affidavit provided by my mother's grand uncle Julius Love, that he could support them. He was a wealthy man, at the time a physician, whose assets would amount to more than a million dollars today. His affidavit was probably the most critical factor in my parents obtaining a visa.

Uncle Love not only provided an affadavit that he would be responsible for them financially, but he also asked that my parents change their name from Wolkowicz to "Love," and that my father, as his "adopted son," eventually take over his medical practice. My parents agreed to all this. The letters sent to them in the States beginning in April 1938 were addressed to Michael and Halina Love.[1]

Settling in Philadelphia

Their home for two years was located in Uncle Love's brick, four-story Victorian house at 315 Pine Street in Philadelphia, the old, gentrified center of the city, today still an upscale neighborhood. The house, which no longer exists, was located directly across the street from the oldest Jewish Cemetery in the city. However, at the time my parents arrived, Jews did not live in significant numbers in this elegant Philadelphia neighborhood.

My parents had one room on the fourth floor, and they were dependent on Uncle Love for a weekly allowance to travel to work or English classes. They had no money when they arrived, and their parents were not in a position to help them. Indeed, they needed to help their parents who had lost their livelihoods and most of their assets in the 1930s depression, so devastating for Poland. They immediately enrolled in a free evening English language class for immigrants held at Boys' Central High School. The plan that my father would take over Uncle Love's practice, however, was not to be.

My father tried to persuade the Pennsylvania Medical Board that he was a credentialed ophthalmologist. After much correspondence, including letters of endorsement from his supervisors in the two French hospitals where he worked, and documents listing the courses in medicine that he took and passed, he was told he must repeat his internship and also pass all of his licensing boards again in the U.S. At the time this was standard American practice for doctors trained in other countries.

My father found a position at Roxborough Memorial Hospital, where his supervising physician, like his mentor in France, was a woman. And like his supervisor in France, Dr. Delthil, she was a supportive and excellent mentor. Throughout his life, my father felt deeply indebted to both of these women. Their impact on him made him a feminist, firmly believing in the potential of women to be leaders in medicine.

Although a wealthy man, Uncle Love did not offer any support besides a room and meals. My mother had to find employment immediately since as an intern my father earned almost nothing; she became my parents' main support. After several failed attempts to assist her cousin Adek in Poland in his proposed business venture to export "fashionable Polish scarves and kerchiefs" to Philadelphia and New York City, my mother tried to find work making elegant women's leather gloves. This was a craft in which she had become expert in France. None of these business ventures succeeded, and she ended up tutoring Americans in French.

Her first student was studying opera at the Curtis Institute of Music, which, like Julliard in New York City, enrolled only the truly gifted. An up and coming opera singer, he was African American—certainly a person of tremendous courage and talent given all the racist barriers he encountered. An opera lover, my mother and he got along well and enjoyed their lessons together. He was probably the first person of color with whom she became acquainted, and this experience deeply influenced her aversion to the racism she witnessed in the United States.

Despite their lack of resources, my parents begin to make a life for themselves. Another couple, considerably older than they, were also bilingual in French and Polish. They had a sixteen-year-old daughter, Josie, who became very attached to my parents. Even in her nineties, Josie still related stories about my parents. She remembered that the first time they visited Josie and her parents in North Philadelphia, they walked there and back to their room on Pine Street because they could not afford carfare. The distance is about 10 miles each way. This story speaks to their determination to make friends in the States. Too proud to talk about their financial circumstances, my parents were eager to make friends. This friendship and others made then lasted throughout their lives.

Although they corresponded regularly with their parents, they also hid their circumstances from them and other relatives in Lodz. But my mother's parents and her uncle Artek immediately sensed from their letters that something was wrong.

Letters From Home

My grandfather wrote immediately after their departure.

Lodz, May 11, 1938

My most beloved children,

We received your letters. I understand very well, that until everything will settle and until you find yourself under new circumstances, it is hard to judge your situation. I can tell you one thing my dearest ones: it is horribly bad here, and no matter how it is there right now, I am sure that you will be happy, and that everything will be fine. And when the moral aspect is concerned, there is no doubt, that the situation over there is not even comparable with the one here.

I know uncle very well, and know that he is an unusually good and decent person. As far as my health is concerned, mother exaggerates. I think that I lost my appetite, eat very little and feel weak because of my accursed nerves. But I think it will improve. The most important thing is that you write often, a lot, and the truth. We so much want to know everything about you. I am sure that everything will be well with you soon.

I wish you all the best, most of all health. I congratulate you and give best wishes to Mikhalek [my father's nickname]. I suspect that this letter will be delayed, but our correspondence did not settle into a routine yet.

I kiss you very, very tenderly. Your loving,
Sasha

My grandmother added a postscript:

Dear Children,

We had a letter from Kuba[2] yesterday. There is no happier man than he. Unfortunately, he could not afford to come and greet you when you arrived. He will come in June or July. Do everything to receive him especially nicely and kindly. I kiss you very tenderly one more time.

MR

She adds at the end in Yiddish: "Write, write, write." These are the words of a popular Yiddish film, *A brivele der mamen* [A Letter to your Mama]. The film is about a son who leaves Europe for America, is almost reunited with his mother, but something happens and it never occurs. I quote the words from a song that opens the film because its emotional tone is so similar to my grandmother's:

> A letter to your mother
> You should not omit
> Write quickly, my beloved child
> Give her a consolation.
> Mother will read your letter and
> be soothed.
> You'll heal her pain, her bitter heart
> And renew her soul.[3]

In his October 28, 1938, letter, my grandfather notes:

What is going on with you my dearest children? There is something strange in your letters, but I hope that all will smooth out and be well.

My mother's uncle Artek, with whom my mother was very close, writes similarly, suspecting something not quite right:

Lodz, September 11, 1938

My dear Halutka,

I received your letter addressed to me with parts for your parents, and I hurry to answer you. First of all, I have to calm you down when it comes to me. It was unnecessary for mother to write you about this accident of mine. I am completely healthy, although the accident was rather unpleasant. Please do forget this matter, especially since there are more serious troubles. I have in mind the health of your father. Sasha looks and feels bad. The doctor diagnoses a serious weakening of the heart. Because of his heart his legs swell all the time. He doesn't have appetite either. Recently, he looks a little better. The injection he is taking is helping him a lot. But unfortunately, I cannot see a big improvement.

It would be good my dears if you could take your parents to America. I understand that you desire this as well, so we must wait patiently.

Your letter dear Halutka made me worry. It's a great pity that you have to go through the difficult and thorny American school of life till you stand on your own, strong feet. But I am sure, I am positive that you will do well there, and then you will bring your parents, and maybe my Marchelek [his son]. Because of the fact that your letters to your parents are, let me say "made up," I am asking you to write honest letters to my address, at least once a month. Is it possible to write to you openly, meaning that letters will not be read by undesirable people?

I worry that the legalization of Mikhal's diploma must take so long, but you are still young [my father was 28 years old and my mother was 30] and everything will be well, the most important thing is to keep yourselves strong and be hopeful. I have always believed and still do in your tenacity, your intrepidness, and your energy.

Recently we haven't had any news from Pepka, Tania, Nunia, and Lolek.[4] Does Uncle receive letters from them? I worry about them a lot.

I received a letter from Fredizio[5] today. He is presently on a week long training. They offered him a better post in Stanislawow,[6] also as a principal of a vocational school. He already accepted and at the beginning of the school year is moving to S. I think his decision is the right one because the town is larger and the opportunities more frequent.

Marchelek is developing really well. He rides a two-wheel bicycle beautifully and in general he behaves well.

Please send Uncle greetings from me and my family and tell him that I am waiting impatiently for his letter.

I kiss you very, very tenderly,
Artek

My grandfather Sasha was indeed very sick and his condition worsened quickly. Nine days before he died he wrote to my mother. These are the last words my mother received from her father.

Kolumna[7]

November 23, 1938

My most beloved and dearest children,

We received your nice and dear letter. I would so much like for Mikhal to settle professionally, and I really wouldn't want him to be outside of Philadelphia.[8]

My dearest, most beloved little child, don't worry so much about us: I feel much better and we are managing financially. I don't want you to work so much because of us. Halusia, "Rome was not built in a day"; so you also have some patience. I am happy that you are in America. I am sure you read what happens in Europe. Write us often and plenty, but most of all, don't worry when it comes to us.

I kiss you most tenderly,
Your loving and missing you Sasha

On December 2, 1938, my grandfather died at the age of 56. In Artek's condolence letter, I am struck by his description of my grandfather's emotional availability and openness, something that my parents often mentioned. Artek singles him out above all others as the one person with whom he could share his deepest feelings.

Lodz, December 20, 1938

My dear beloved Halinka,

What we all feared so much finally happened. Your poor father and our beloved brother parted with this life on December 2, at 4 p.m. My dear, poor Halutka! It's hard, it's very hard for me to write to you in this moment. I would like to be together with you, to hold you and then speak, but what is one to do when we are divided by such huge terrible space.

I wrote to you my Galinochka (as Sasha always called you) in my previous letter, that pneumonia added to the very serious illness of your father, and that the doctors did not have high hopes, and then the illness started progressing so fast, that almost immediately after diagnosis was stated, the death came. Poor Sasha died on Friday, December 2nd in Kolumna, at the time when I, together with Doctor Tennenbaum, set out by car from Lodz. We did not find him among the living any more.

This misfortune happened so fast and so unexpectedly. Death came very fast.

You, my dear Halutka, during your last stay in Lodz most likely noticed these serious changes in your father's health, especially the change in his mood. And you must know that he knew how to keep up appearances. After your departure, Halutka, your father was wilting away. He intuited that he would never see you again, and usually when I tried to calm him down by saying that he has to be healthy because he still has a journey to his children, whom he loves so much, and that over there, with you, his life will become different — better and easier. To these words of mine, he just waved his hand in a very pessimistic gesture, and in his eyes, one could see a smirk, testifying to the doubt with which he took my words.

Yes, my dear Halutka, Sasha suffered a lot in recent times, and it was hard to look at him. Mom holds herself pretty bravely, but she looks really bad, and we are trying to do everything to make her fate bearable. The funeral took place on Sunday, December 4th. Janek and Roza[9] came from Warsaw, Fredzio from Stanislawow. It won't be much help to you, but the funeral was impressive. All friends and acquaintances came to give the last greetings to our beloved Sasha.

I miss him very much. After all, he was the only adult to whom I could turn for advice, or with whom, I could speak from the heart.[10] I will feel often the absence of this good-hearted, beloved, "edgy" man. And you Halutka, you have to take hold of yourself and think about your mother, who should especially now, be together with you. I am sure that Mikhal, Aunt and Uncle will try, as much as possible, to calm you in this very hard situation in which you find yourself. I ask you Halutka, don't leave me without information about you and try to bravely face this huge, terrible pain.

My whole family is sending you their deepest condolences.

I kiss you very, very tenderly,
Your loving Artek

My grandmother delayed her letter until she was able to gather herself together to write on January 15, 1939.

My dearest, beloved children,

My dearest Halusia, my child, you already know what a terrible blow we suffered. We lost our most beloved Father. Our sun has set forever. I feel better now, my dear orphaned girl, we are crying together. My eyes cannot stop crying. I can't accept this terrible truth.

Nothing in the world makes me happy, my heart is breaking, I am so lonely. If I at least had you, my dearest children, we could cry together and despair. Dear Halunia, I have you alone in this world. Be strong, our only, beloved daughter. Father loved you so much, didn't part with your photograph, kissed it and blessed you, my dear children, so much that surely you will be very happy in your life.

As for you Halus, be understanding. You are young. Father will not rise from his grave, and you have a good, loving husband. You must live and be healthy for dear Mikhalek, for your aged beyond her years mother, who has only you, my children, since father's death. We are not the first and not the last ones in our sorrow. Halunia, take hold of yourself for me.

I am giving away our apartment. I can't live here now. I feel the wind of bitterness and sorrow from this apartment, once bathed in sun and happiness. I took a room in the same building, but I can't stay there either. I spend whole days at the pension, but I can't find myself there either.[11] I feel bad here as well. Guests want to have fun, I want to cry.

Dora and Abram [her sister and brother-in- law] *asked me to stay at their place, but what do I do, I don't have my own room there, and when the guests come I would have to give up my room. I will probably pay at least 60 zloty a month and have my own room there. I don't know how to organize it. I don't need a household, Halusia doesn't need it either, but to throw it all away — one could furnish a six room apartment with all this stufi. But this is a trifle. There is no more Father, no more sun.*

Finally I forgot to tell you, my children that the funeral was extremely beautiful. Father was buried next to his dear father. There were beautiful speeches in Polish and Yiddish. They were praising father, as he deserved to be praised. Half the town was there, a lot of young people, a choir and cantor. But you my dear children were not there. And so this is how I said good-bye to him.

My children, I know you so much want to take me to be with you. I can't even think about leaving father's grave. This cemetery grounds me. And I so much want Hala to come visit me, but it is impossible.

I kiss you tenderly. Write to your loving, longing mother.

The relationship between my grandmother and her sister Dora deteriorated rapidly. Soon my grandmother's determination to stay in Poland shifted, and she began to inquire about emigrating to the U.S.

But she is hesitant to write to Uncle Love from whom she heard not one word of condolence.

March 1, 1939,

There is no way out of it. I have to ask uncle meekly for his help...I will sell the house because I could operate with that money.[12] The administrator writes that there are people interested in it already. And how long could it take such emigration from here? How long does it take to get a visa? And what about money? The journey costs so much. I am sure you will inform me about everything.

She is still concerned that things have not worked out as anticipated, that my father has not taken over Uncle Love's practice:

> *How do you feel my children? Write me how things are with you, what is uncle's attitude towards you. After all uncle wanted to settle Mikhal in, he wanted Mikhal to work in his practice because he can't do it himself anymore, and it appears that you have nothing in common with him. Doesn't uncle try to help you in your new life? His protection doesn't seem to be of any use? I don't understand it at all. Aren't you in good standing with him so you can pull Mikhal into his practice. I don't understand what is going on with you. You never write honestly about what is going on.*

Once my grandmother made up her mind that the only way she would be happy was to go to her children, she tried to obtain a visa to the U.S. My parents' letters suggest that at first they and my grandmother were hopeful. Uncle Love provided an affadavit regarding his support of his niece (my grandmother) as did my grandmother's brother in Chicago, and she began to make the rounds of consulates.

In the meantime, her survival depended on money that she received from her brother who lived in Chicago and from my mother and father, who regularly sent whatever they could. In her letter of May 10, 1938, she notes, "*Now I can pay my rent, first payment for the room. Then I will give a deposit for the stone for the grave of our dear father.*" She suffered from diabetes, was beginning to lose her eyesight, and wrote to my father to make recommendations on what she should do. Her relationship with her sister and brother-in-law remained difficult. They never wrote a letter of condolence to my mother, and yet complained that my mother never wrote to them. Since my grandmother depended so much on them, she tried to persuade my mother to "be polite" to her Aunt Dora, even if she didn't want to. She spent her days in their pension in Kolumna and took her meals with them.

May 31, 1938,

I am so nervous, I am not sur prised that I have high blood sugar. I simply don't know how to liquidate my possessions. What should I take [she is already assuming that she is going to her children], *where should I leave things in Lodz? Mikhal's parents instead of helping me don't answer me at all, and when they talk to me, his mother says, "What do they need it for. There are nicer things in America. Aunt must have a good household. Why drag it from Lodz?" I feel they are cold.*

The most important thing is that I got an afiidavit from my dearest beloved brother, as far as I can say, a very good one. Now I am waiting for this second one. It's true, it impressed me. I so believed that father and I would go to our dear children together. But this is not God's given fate! This is what religious people say. I have to believe it too.

By June 24, my grandmother had received all of the documents needed from my parents, Uncle Love, and her brother. She also wrote that things were much better with her sister, that they treat her well and "love me very much." Also, their son Adek has moved into the pension with his wife Fela, and my grandmother has fallen in love with their baby, Anitka.

On July 17, 1938, she writes about her trip to Lodz to discuss emigration. She was told to visit the American Jewish Joint Distribution Committee.[13] In her letter she refers to it as "A Society for Helping Immigrants."

I was received by a director of the Society, most likely an attorney. He translated all three afiidavits. He said, "Documents from Uncle [Love] are most important." Kuba [her brother Jakob/Jack] doesn't have money in the bank, and this is very important. The quota for immigrants is full. One needs to wait at least three years. The quota does not include children traveling to parents, parents traveling to children, a wife traveling to husband and vice versa.[14]

She suggests that they write to Washington [she provides an address] to the JDC to obtain a "preferential visa," one that is not limited by the quota.

She continues,

He [the head of the organization] already wanted to keep those papers and to register me. I, on the other hand, started to feel sick to my stomach, knowing that immigration is closed for the next three to four years, and that he has hope that you can obtain documents for me to leave since I am alone, and my husband died recently, and that you desire your mother with you. He wanted to register me.

I listened carefully and said "I will not register, because I want to go personally to the Consul." I said I had protections (I had in mind Janek).[15] I decided to go to Warsaw on Wednesday, July 19th of this week.

Truth to be told, this director in Lodz did not advise me to go there. He said that Consul may only do harm to my case—take the afiidavit and do nothing.[16] *Adek* [her nephew] *laughed at this, saying "I prefer to go to the head than to the … [left blank to refer to the "ass," meaning the least important]." These are my first steps. I will write you immediately from Warsaw to tell you how things stand. Janek is going for vacation on July 25, and I want to catch him before that. Perhaps he will be willing to help me. So far this immigration is not going so easily.*

She also writes that she received the check from my parents. *It came to 106 zlotys and 36 groszy.*[17] *Thank you very much for remembering me. I am touched that you care about me so much.*

My grandmother then touches on what she understands of my parents' status in Uncle Love's home:

Dear children, you already have "Love" as your last name. Why do the documents state "Wolkowicz?"

She also writes about the state of her health:

I don't see very well, but I am not changing my glasses because I was told to stay with the same ones. I get mad, when I use the wrong thread to sew black things, and when my knitting doesn't come out so well. Doctor [she means my father] *it's hard for me to read in the evenings. I thought I was going to see you and that you would cure me, but now, I see that's not such an easy thing, so I get nervous because of this.*

And she returns to the issue of my parents being adopted by Uncle Love:

Several times I wanted to ask you why you write "Wolkowicz" in all documents, addressee, etc. Here in Kolumna, when they see the addressee "Wolkowicz," they ask me sarcastically, "It must be some mistake on your part." After all it would be good to have "Love" as your name. It is probably very important for Michael's practice.

I have always been proud of my parents' decision to "go it alone," especially because their uncle did not treat them in the way they expected. They were finding that they could do this. From my grandmother's point of view, however, it was clear that a Jewish name would handicap my parents and that it was not a wise decision on their part to remain a "Wolkowicz" and to forego Uncle Love's offer to take over his practice, his name, and ultimately his wealth which was substantial. So my parents' decision was a brave one since they literally had nothing. It was clearly based on a desire for independence and for proving to themselves that they could make it on their own without being beholden to anyone.

On September 1, 1939, my grandmother writes:

In my last letter, I promised you to write from Warsaw, but my business went so badly, that even after my return, I am not in a hurry to write you about it. I don't feel like returning to this subject, but after all, I have to present how things stand.

I went to see the Consul in Warsaw and asked Janek to go with me, but he didn't have time because it was two days before his departure to the spa in Morszyn. He recommended his friend, a refugee from Berlin, who accompanied me everywhere, a very nice man. We went to see the Consul. I had all my documents with me. The Consul did not see me at all. He doesn't see people. Only his secretary does. He read all my papers, everything was in order, but he told me only children have the right to travel to their parents, and are not included in the quota. I was told the same thing in Lodz. If the children receive the right in Washington to take their widowed mother to her only daughter, then Uncle's documents will be very helpful. For now, no documents will help. I must receive this document from you to achieve the status of a "privileged" one in the quota.

The secretary told me that it wouldn't make sense for me to register now, because it will take many years because the Polish quota has been frozen for five or six years. From there, we went to an Emigration Society and from there they sent me to the Joint Committee (JDC) in Warsaw. Full circle. You, my children, have to organize over there all kinds of "privileged" documents. I can't do anything here. You understand how sad this makes me feel. I am a nice, welcomed guest everywhere because I was about to emigrate. It was a matter of months. Now it begins again: finding a room for the winter, my wandering from place to place. I must organize myself anew, lonely, without strength. I believe that my fate is really harsh.

How is your health my dearest children?

Mikhal doesn't write me much. I so like his letters. Halus, do you have enough clothing. Do you buy yourselves some things. Halus, there are such beautiful cotton beach dresses here. Should I have one made for you. They are not expensive.

I am also sending you Anitka's photograph. Adek and his wife gave it to me to send to you. She is a wonderful child. I love her a lot. Write them already! And tell them that you are waiting for an opportunity to send her a beautiful American doll, the one I wrote you about.

Be healthy and happy. I hug and kiss you.

Missing you,
mom

The War Begins

This was the last uncensored letter that my grandmother ever wrote. World War II started on September 1, 1939, when the Germans invaded Poland.

Since the war began in the north, in Danzig, the first city bombed and captured, my grandmother obviously was not aware of the catastrophe that was unfolding when she wrote this letter. Certainly by the end of this day, she knew. Five months were to pass before she was able to communicate again with her children, this time with a few clearly censored lines, hiding all but the fact that she, Dora, Abram, and their children and grandchild were alive, as were Artek and his family.

I have thought many times about this last letter of September 1, 1939, written the day the Nazis attacked Poland while the rest of the world watched and waited. She must not yet have known what was happening, living as she did in the country outside of a major city. I have thought about how she refrained from expressing what must have been crushing disappointment that she could not emigrate in the foreseeable future. As a parent she needed to be "parental," and not burden her children, whose lives she realized were not easy, with her disappointment. But she let them know she felt she had become a burden on others. She had no money and was dependent on the good will of relatives and anything my parents were able to send. Her relationship with her sister was strained. And her health was not good. If indeed emigration was not possible for another five or six years, she probably imagined she might not live that long, that she might never see her daughter and son-in-law again.

And yet in this dark moment, before she knew that World War II had started, before she became another "jude" to be disposed of, she wanted her daughter to have a "beautiful cotton beach dress," to imagine her having pleasure during the summer months. She wanted her to look beautiful and feel good. She wanted my parents to buy a doll for her grandniece Anitka. She was clearly hoping to be a grandmother, and Anitka was for her the substitute for the grandchild of her dreams. And she wanted my parents to "be nice" to her nephew Adek and his wife Fela [Felicia] by buying Anitka an American doll, something special.

The story of the marriage of Adek and Fela is one that I discovered on my trip to Lodz in 2012. Hoping to find Anitka in Poland, I visited Lodz's Civil Records office to look for her mother's maiden name. I learned that Fela was not Jewish and that the couple decided to be married by a priest in a church in order to baptize Anitka and to have her officially registered as Christian. They had had a Jewish wedding several years earlier, but only a "church" wedding would be recorded in Civil Records. The "wedding" took place in December 1938 several months after Anitka's birth.

Soon after this, the family fled to Warsaw before the Lodz Ghetto was established in May 1940. In a letter to my parents written from the Warsaw Ghetto, Adek and Fela enclosed a photo of Anitka.

According to information my parents received after the war, both Adek and Fela were shot and killed while trying to escape the Warsaw Ghetto. However, Anitka was given to someone outside the ghetto to be cared for. My parents tried to locate her after the war but were not successful.

As soon as the Polish government officially surrendered on September 27, 1939, after huge losses of both civilians and soldiers, the Germans divided Poland into two territories. The north and west sector of which Lodz was part was directly incorporated into Germany as the "Neue Reich." The larger central and southern part of Poland, which included Warsaw, was constituted as the "General Gouvernement." No longer governed by civil law, both areas were constituted as Work Areas (Arbeitsberiech) with martial law enforced. For any crimes there was only death or a concentration camp once the camps were established.

The Germans immediately began implementing a racial classification system with privileges such as food rations doled out accordingly. Germans born in Germany, known as *Reichsdeutsche*, were the most privileged; the *Volksdeutsche* (German nationals who were not born in Germany but could prove they were German three generations back) were the second category; *Nichtdeutsche* (non-Germans) applied to Poles; and *Juden*, to Jews. All able-bodied were expected to work, and their food allowance was measured in calories based on their "race" and productivity. Non-productive Jews received no food allowance. Racial apartheid was quickly enforced in all public places — parks, trams, "better shops and hotels," where signs that read *Nur fur Deutsche* [For Germans Only] were posted.

Immediately after Lodz was occupied on September 8, 1939, Jews were subjected to brutal harassment on the streets if they wore the traditional dress that marked them. They were stripped of clothes, sometimes forced to dance in the streets as people jeered and laughed, and made to do the most menial and filthy work in public view. Beards were shaved.

Goebbels visited Lodz in October 1939. In his diary he noted:

> *Lodz itself is a hideous city. Drive through the Ghetto* [he is referring to the section called Baluty inhabited mainly by working class and poor Jews]. *It is indescribable. These are not human beings, they are animals. For this reason, our task is no longer humanitarian, but surgical. Steps must be taken here, and they must be radical ones. Make no mistake about it.*[18]

Throughout the fall, citizens were shot and tortured. On November 1, Jewish artists, writers, and politicians who frequented the fashionable Astoria Café on Piotrkowska Street were hauled out and told to appear the next day at the offices of the Gestapo. All were taken away to the nearby Legniewnicki Woods, and 15 were shot while six others were forced to dig their graves. Shortly afterwards on November 8, Lodz was declared a German city, the name changed to Lodsch and later to Litzmannstadt. The initial plan in the Germanizing of Lodz was to remove a sizeable number of Poles and Jews. But this plan proved logistically impossible. In the meantime, Jews began to flee the city in considerable numbers.

On November 10, the first of the four main synagogues in Lodz was burned to the ground. Members of the Jewish Council, which governed the Jews of Lodz in matters concerning social welfare, were taken away to an improvised concentration camp, horribly tortured, and all but a handful, killed.

On November 14, all Jews in the city were forced to outfit themselves with the armbands with the star of David in the specified "Jewish yellow" color, which they were to wear at all times. From this time forward Piotrkowska Street, the main thoroughfare, near the apartment buildings where both of my parents grew up, was off limits to Jews. And *a* curfew was established that barred Jews from being on the streets from 5 p.m. until 8 a.m. the next morning.

Once these decisions were made, some of the humiliating direct harassment of Jews in the streets ceased, and the Germans focused on moving non-Jewish citizens out of the area that had been agreed-upon as the site for the Jewish Ghetto. The notion of a separate area was publically justified because of the supposed unsanitary conditions in which Jews were said to live and the dangers from infections, spotted fever being among those mentioned, for the rest of the population. Jews were seen as an "infectious disorder" to be contained.

In fact, the greatest infectious danger at the time was tuberculosis. The Germans discovered that Jews had a lower infection rate than the rest of the population due, they reasoned, to the fact that Jews did not perform manual labor and therefore were not as vulnerable to TB.

The site of the ghetto was to be an enlarged area based on the Baluty neighborhood of Lodz where the poorest Jews lived. All non-Jews from this area were to be moved to other areas of the city, and compensated for their dwellings while the organization of the ghetto was planned. The planning included its leadership, governance, and ways it could be made economically beneficial to the German war effort while temporarily containing the Jewish population of the city. Germans were clear that this was a temporary move awaiting further decisions about the dispensation of Jews in Poland.

From January 1940 to May 1940 when the Lodz Ghetto was established, three brief, censored postcards reached my parents, each one from a different address. All Jewish possessions and assets had been confiscated by the time the first letter arrived, and able-bodied Jews were conscripted into forced labor. The family was forced from one lodging to the next, and their mail was not getting through to my parents. It is clear from the three postcards that my parents received before the establishment of the Lodz Ghetto in May 1940 that family members were on the move from one living space to the next. It was also clear from my grandmother's correspondence that if you had the means to get out of Lodz, Warsaw, which was not incorporated into Germany, was considered the better option.

The three postcards from January to March 1940 which reached my parents were clearly censored.

The first one from January 21, 1940. The sender is Maria (a Germanized version of my grandmother's name, which was Mera) Rozin.

> *My dearest children, aunt and uncle,*
>
> *I am writing to you for the second time already. I am waiting for your dear letter to learn how you are doing. I am healthy and so are Aunt Dora, Uncle Abram, Fela, Adek, and Anitka. Hela, Marchelek and Artek are also doing well. We are staying together. I kiss you and greet you from the bottom of my heart.*
>
> *Your mother,*
> *Maria Rozin*

The family mentioned included seven adults and two children living together: my grandmother, her sister Dora and her husband Abram, her sister's son Adek and his wife Fela and child Anitka, and my grandfather's brother Artek and his wife Ester and child Marchelek. It is clear that Jews were no longer in possession of their homes, were crowded into whatever spaces were allotted, and wrote what would pass the censors. The stamps are German ones. And the street address is the German version of Piotrkowska, now Petrikauerstrasse.

A similar postcard was mailed on February 15 from another address. This postcard seems to have been rerouted multiple times; on March 15 it reached Philadelphia. In this card, my grandmother says it is her "fourth" card. Again, she says what is possible under censorship:

> *My dearest Uncle, Aunt, and the Children,*
>
> *I keep writing and writing without getting a response. I am mailing you the fourth card, registered like the first ones. I would like to know what is going on with you, whether you are healthy and happy.*
>
> > *We are all healthy. I am staying with Abram and Dora and I am healthy. Mikhal's parents are in Lodz. They write to you using my address. They are healthy. We are all longingly awaiting your letters. Adek, Fela and the lovely child Anitka are in Warsaw and they are healthy. Aunt Luba[19] is very sick. She lives with her children in Warsaw and she writes to me from Warsaw via the American consul. Please write to dearest Jakob [her brother] in Chicago. I am not sure I have the right address for him. I have written him three cards. I have my afiidavit from you. I kiss and hug you a thousand fold.*
>
> *Your loving and missing you mom and niece.*

At this point, since Warsaw is looking better than Lodz, the family has split, with Adek, Fela, and Anitka, as well as Artek, Ester, and Marchelek going to Warsaw.

The last postcard my parents received from outside the Lodz Ghetto was dated March 11, 1940. It was registered on April 2, 1940. This time there is no return address except the "Jewish Congregation."

> *My dearest children, uncle and aunt,*
>
> *I am writing my twelfth letter to you but unfortunately I haven't received any responses from you yet. Mikhal's parents received a letter through the*

Red Cross (I had already let you know about it.) I didn't read it and therefore I am very uneasy whether or not you are all healthy and whether you keep a secret from me. We are all healthy. I live with Dora and Abram. Adek and his family are in Warsaw. Mikhal's parents are healthy and we live close to them. Henri [married to Tania, her sister-in- law] *keeps writing to me and sent me a package with butter via post from Riga. I was very touched with his thoughtfulness. Please write to him:* [address is given in Riga, Latvia]. *How are you doing my dear ones, are you all healthy. Your dear uncle* [she means her brother Jack in Chicago] *writes to me through the Red Cross, Jewish Congregation. Please write to me using Adek's Warsaw address* [which she provides].

This is all from us. Please write often. Perhaps I will finally get a letter from you.

Kisses and hugs,
Your loving Maria.

Abram and Dora also greet and kiss you from the bottom of their heart.

These last three postcards from my grandmother are filled with emotion that cannot be expressed, fear of abandonment by her children, and sadness at the splitting of the family, with those younger and possessing more resources fleeing to Warsaw, where it appeared there was less pillaging and terror.

Days and months pass without her hearing from anyone until the final move to the Lodz Ghetto in May 1940, where my grandmother would die from starvation, separated from those closest and dearest.

Endnotes

1 Julius Love's Polish name was Milewsky, the maiden name of my maternal great grandmother, which roughly translates into English as "love." In Polish "milowac" means to love, to have a passion for.

2 Nickname for her brother Jakob, who went by John or Jack in the States.

3 Translation by Elizabeth Kosakowska.

4 His three sisters and next-to-youngest brother who live in the Soviet Union at this time. Lolek had probably already died during Stalin's purge of the Polish Community Party.

5 The youngest brother, who was studying engineering.

6 A town near Warsaw.

7 A small town and vacation spot outside of Lodz, where my grandmother's sister Dora owned and ran a pension. My grandparents found an apartment there and were living there except for the visits to the hospital in Lodz where Sasha was being treated.

8 Because my parents were unhappy in Philadelphia, they were considering a move to New York City.

9 Janek was the oldest brother and Roza was his wife.

10 The words "from the heart" were written in Russian "po dusham" which literally translates as "soul to soul."

11 She is referring to her sister's vacation pension in Kolumna.

12 My grandmother co-owned a house in Suwalki with her sister and brother-in-law. She was dependent on her brother-in-law to make the sale.

13 In the letter, my grandmother abbreviates the committee as JEAZA. I assume it was the American Joint Distribution Committee (usually referred to as JDC), but it may have been another organization.

14 She means that these are allowed relatives that are not included in the quota.

15 The oldest brother in the Rozin family and a judge. My grandmother was not fond of him or his wife.

16 This was accurate. U.S. consuls were more often likely to limit immigration even when legally allowed as were parents of children already in the States. Many were anti- Semitic or generally opposed to having immigrants such as Eastern European Jews.

17 Approximately $33 in U.S dollars.

18 Horwitz, Ghettostadt: *Lodz and the Making of a Nazi City*, 22.

19 I do not know this relative or how she was related to my parents.

Chapter 4

Voices of Despair — Letters from the Lodz Ghetto, 1940–1942

For My Grandmother:

33 Ciesielska, apt. 2

*I see you walking thin and bent
a tattered coat pulled tight against
the cold
Not glancing right or left,
no eye contact wanted*

*I hear you now
your words in tiny script
on yellowing postcards
a Nazi swastika next to
Return address:
33 Ciesielska, apt. 2*

*Who listened then?
A voice of despair,
A cry of hunger,
A mother's concern
Hopeful and hopeless
I hear you now
Who heard you then?*

The second of three children, my grandmother, Mera Kagan Rozin,[1] was born in the town of Suwalki[2] on May 22, 1884. She died in the Lodz Ghetto on September 28, 1942, at the age of 58.

According to my grandmother's death certificate, the cause of death was "malnutrition," the leading cause of death in the ghetto after heart disease and tuberculosis and a major contributor to these two causes of death. By May 1942, the food rations for the Lodz Ghetto amounted to 1,100 calories a day, and less for the unemployed like my grandmother.[3]

My grandmother wrote 39 "postcards" from the Lodz Ghetto to my parents living in Philadelphia—the first on May 23, 1940, and the final one on June 12, 1941. On June 22, 1941, the Germans invaded the Soviet Union. By December 11, 1941, four days after the bombing of Pearl Harbor by the Japanese, the Germans declared war on the United States. Certainly, at that point, no further correspondence with residents of the U.S. was possible.

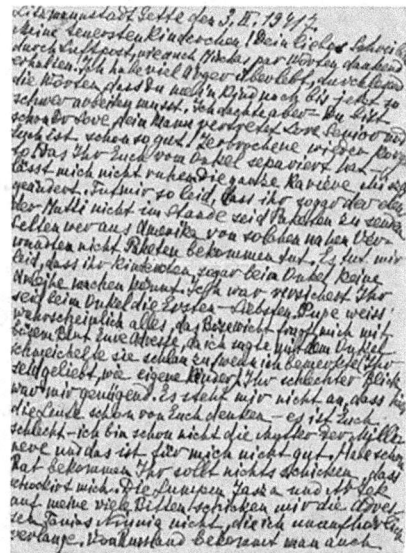

Cards from Lodz Ghetto. February 3, 1941.
From my grandmother to my parents. This card is
addressed to their home in Philadelphia.

Except for the first few, the postcards were written in German, a language that my grandmother learned in the gymnasium that she attended. According to the translator of her postcards, she was a competent writer in German. Her ability to write in German made it easier to pass censorship although both sending and receiving mail was always erratic, subject to the whims and censorship of German officials.

In reading my grandmother's postcards, I immersed myself in the physical realities of her existence as well the emotional torment that she felt but could not openly express in postcards—the possibility of never seeing her children again and her feeling of abandonment when she didn't receive letters. Drawing on the vast amount of research on and documentation of the Lodz Ghetto, I have tried to provide the background and context for her letters. The Lodz Ghetto has been extensively researched because documents describing it were concealed and preserved in the last days of the ghetto's existence. No other ghetto has been documented in this way. The internal documentation was done by a team of 15 journalists, writers, economists, and other members of the intelligentsia who constituted an archives department. The *Chronicle of the Lodz Ghetto* began on January 21, 1941. Until September 1, 1942, it was written in Polish; then until July 30, 1944, in German.

The writers adopted the following principle: "Since it is not possible to write about those who commit the crimes, we will speak of their victims, and in some detail."[4] Lucjan Dobroszski, the editor of the English version, describes it as "reminiscent of the medieval chronicles written in besieged towns that were doomed by destruction and, on the other hand, of a censored contemporary newspaper, not to be read by anyone except those who wrote it."[5]

Establishing the Lodz Ghetto

After the Polish Government surrendered to the Germans in October 1939, Poland was divided into two spheres. Wartheland in the west was incorporated into the German Reich with the intention of settling this part of Poland exclusively with Germans. The General Gouvernement, in the east, which included Warsaw, was to be the area in which Poles would eventually be settled. While both areas were subject to the same loss of civil liberties, deportations, and killings, there was a difference in how the Germans viewed Wartheland, and Lodz, above all.

Lodz was intended to become the model German town of the future, from which all Jews would be expelled. However the logistical issues of relocating

233,000 Jews were great, and ultimately a decision was made to temporarily enclose the Jews of Lodz, as well as those in other towns in confined areas separate from the German and Polish populations. Since Lodz was an industrial city, it would function as something akin to a forced labor camp in producing goods for the German army.

Because of the sadistic acts of German soldiers in Lodz immediately after the Polish surrender, those Jews who could, fled. Mainly, these were affluent families and the intelligentsia. Those left behind — 164,000 out of a total of 233,000 Jews who resided in Lodz before the war-- represented a cross-section of Jewish society. Mainly however, "Those remaining were largely the poor and those unable to make their escape — the elderly."[6]

In April 1940, Lodz was renamed Litzmannstadt after a German World War I commander, who was also a Nazi supporter. The ghetto was intended to be temporary; Jewish workers would pay for the maintenance of the ghetto through their labor. Although intended to be temporary, the ghetto outlived all the other Polish ghettos because of its continued usefulness to the German war effort.

The area chosen for the ghetto, Baluty and the Old Town, included the two sections of Lodz where the poorest of the Jewish population lived. The Old Town was the original area of Lodz, which was the Jewish district until 1861. These two areas were the most impoverished neighborhoods in Lodz.[7] Of the 31,962 dwellings, 89 percent consisted of two rooms, and 95 percent had no water pipes or sewage disposal.[8] The area of the ghetto was 4.1 square kilometers, but actual living space was limited to 2.4 square kilometers. To give an idea of the ensuing crowding, before the war 10,248 lived on one square kilometer in this area; in the Lodz Ghetto the number was 68,000 per square kilometer.[9]

The Lodz Ghetto was distinctive in that unlike other ghettos "it was hermetically sealed, impregnable and isolated."[10] In his discussion of the Lodz Ghetto Isaiah Trunk explains that it was the only ghetto in which smuggling was impossible. Two units of police guarded it at all times--the Jewish police within and the Germans on the outside. In general, unlike the Warsaw Ghetto, contact with the outside world was impossible. There were no newspapers allowed from the outside, and radios were almost nonexistent and hidden. Anyone who tried to escape was shot on the spot by the German soldiers who ringed the ghetto at all times.

Within the ghetto, Jews were entirely dependent on food supplies provided by Germans. All goods manufactured in the ghetto were for German use; the currency, called "rumki" by the inhabitants, was useless on the outside. Jews who entered the ghetto were allowed one suitcase that they could carry without assistance. They were forced to sell most of their personal property, including furniture and jewelry, and to give over any savings that they held in banks to the ghetto authorities.

The ghetto was governed by a Judenrat, a Jewish council that was introduced into all of the ghettos of Poland.

Mordechai Chaim Rumkovski, was Chairman of the Lodz Judenrat and known as the Judenalteste (Elder of the Jews). He appointed all of the members of the Judenrat and the heads of the various public offices. All were personally responsible to him. He essentially had total governing power within the ghetto but was always beholden to his German superiors. To underscore and ridicule his authority, he was called "King Chaim" by many.

The Nazis' ingenious solution to governance in all their conquered territories was to force the Judenrat to carry out Nazi orders, thus channeling discontent to the Jewish administration rather than to the Germans. However, in no other ghetto was control so complete and unchallenged as in the Lodz Ghetto. This is not to say that internal resistance didn't occur. The ghetto was composed of the full continuum of political parties among Jews– Communists, members of the Bund, Socialists, and the various Zionist groups, as well as several Orthodox Jewish parties–and because the resistance was internal, it was up to Jewish authorities appointed by the Germans to suppress it. There were numerous prolonged strikes and demonstrations. However, in no instance did resistance result in revolt as it did in the Warsaw Ghetto. The simplest explanation is that nowhere else was any ghetto so completely cut off from its surrounding population, and no ghetto was so profitable for the Germans, which meant there was employment for the able-bodied.

Rumkovski is a controversial figure. He has been viewed by most historians, but not all, as a tool in the hands of the Germans. He had full power to choose all members of his Council of Elders. All Jewish agencies from before the war were dissolved and reassembled under his control. His controlling idea was that if the ghetto produced enough goods for the Germans it would be saved, even though not everyone would be saved. He was the one who enforced the deportations, even when he knew by 1942 that the inhabitants were led to death by gassing with carbon monoxide at Chelmno (before the mass killing technology in Auschwitz-Birkenau had been fully developed).

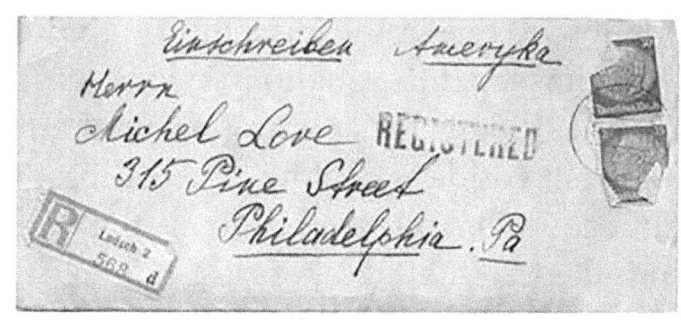

Letter addressed to my father Michel Love

My Grandmother's Location

My grandmother lived at 33 Ciesielska Street, apartment 2. However, she used the German version of the street name—Bleicherweg—on her correspondence until 1941, when she switched to its Polish name. Most of the streets were renamed by the Germans using numbers and letters, boldly displayed in black on yellow, the "Jewish color" used on armbands and later the star pinned to everyone's breast. But my grandmother chose to use the Polish name on her return address—a signal, possibly, to her children of her actual location.

Ciesielska was and is a one-block street that I found easily when I visited the area of Lodz encompassed by the ghetto. My grandmother was one of five in the allotted living space. The inhabitants of their apartment included her sister Dora Polakov, her husband Abram, and his two brothers, Sasha and Boris. When I visited Lodz, the building in which my grandmother and her family lived was no longer standing. One old, unpainted wooden building, typical of the housing in the ghetto, remained on the street. The block where my grandmother lived was very close to the heart of the ghetto, namely the main square, Baluty. This is where Rumkovski resided as well and where the Jewish Ghetto administration and the German Food and Economic Office headed by Hans Biebow was located. It was where Rumkovski delivered speeches, including those announcing deportations.

Ciesielska was also close to one of the main thoroughfares of Lodz, Zgierska Street. Because this street bisected the ghetto in two places, its residents had to cross it via two overhead bridges. In crossing over, ghetto inhabitants could see the lives of non-Jewish residents below proceeding about their business "normally"-a constant reminder to them of life on the "outside," and, for the citizens of Lodz, a reminder that their fate was less horrible than that of the Jews. And finally, it was close to Koscielny Square where the Church of the Virgin Mary was located. The Kripo or criminal police established its headquarters in one of the buildings adjoining the church, and the church itself became the main depository for clothing and personal possessions sent back to be sorted following deportations. The sorting was conducted by ghetto residents.

The Letters: May 23 to December 24, 1940

May 23, 1940

My dearest children![11]

We received your dear letter through Henri[12] *and you cannot imagine what joy I felt on this day, this day in which after such a harsh, long war, after nine months, I finally received living words from the person dearest to me* [my mother wrote the letter]. *Only I worried a lot about the fact that Mikhal did not write a few words in his own hand. But I want to believe that you are healthy and doing well, my dearest ones. I am so happy that you are together with uncle* [her uncle Julius Love who made it possible for my parents to emigrate to the U.S.] *and that you don't feel uneasy with him.*

I am very glad that Mikhal has opened his own practice. I wish you good luck, health and happiness in your young, beautiful life.

I responded to you immediately through Henri, via registered mail [letters sent by registered mail were more likely to get through]. *I am repeating myself in my letter because I am not sure which letter will reach you first. I am as king you don't send* [no word is supplied here because she is referring to money which would have been confiscated]. *I received a notice from the bank in Berlin about receiving 50 RM [Reichs Marks] also on May 18th. sent a receipt to Berlin. I signed 3 papers: 1. Explanation; 2. Receipt 3. Request and I sent it back to Berlin.*

When I will receive the money, I don't know. Thank you very much that you are not forgetting about me. Henri promises to send provisions.

Things with us are as I wrote. I live with Dora and Abram. Sasha and Boris live with us. Jasha, Abram's brother stayed where he was on vacation [my grandmother was obviously hiding his whereabouts since no one was vacationing in the midst of a war], *at the same place where you visited* [she is probably referring to the pension belonging to Dora and Abram which was in Kolumna outside of Lodz]. *Artek* [her brother-in-law] *returned from the POW camp* [he fought in the Polish army and was released after capture] *and lives with our Fredek* [his younger brother]. *I don't know about Janek* [another brother-in-law].[13] *As you know Adek* [son of Dora and Abram] *is in Warsaw.*

We are feeling well. God grant the end of this war and that we will see each other alive.[14] *My dearest children, write as often as you can, and in detail about yourselves and your beloved Uncle. May he be healthy. I kiss you tenderly, most tenderly. I long to hear from Mikhal.*

Mom

I wrote them [she is referring to my father's parents] *that I got your letter.*

Dora adds her postscript in Polish to my parents:

Dear Halusia and Mikhalek! After such a long break, it would seem that one needs to write a copious letter, but unfortunately, it is forbidden to write too much. Considering that Mania wrote so much this time, I will limit myself to wishing you much, much happiness.

I hug and kiss you tenderly,
Love, Dora

Also on May 23, 1940, she writes to her brother Jakob whom she affectionately calls by his nickname, Rudek. The letter is substantially the same as the one above except that she mentions that the letter she received from my mother whom she calls by one of her many nicknames, Galushka came via Henri, her brother-in-law in Riga. This suggests that at this time correspondence with the U.S., although allowed, was very difficult and that the safer way to correspond seemed to be through the Soviet Union, then an ally of Germany. This letter was written in Russian, my grandmother's first language. On the envelope she uses the name

Maria Rozin, not Mera, which was her Russian given name. She mentions that she has written 15 registered letters *"but unfortunately, I didn't get the answer to any of them, but I still think that you were writing to me and the letters will come."*

She also notes that *"Henri has responded to all my letters,"* and she has also heard from Mikhal, my father. *"Henri promises to send packages soon, only he needs foreign currency for that."* She also asks Rudek not to send money.

> *"I beg you, write to me more often, we will get something, and through Henri. Let the children know."*

She signs: *"Your very devoted and loving sister, Mania"* Dora adds:

> *Considering that Mania wants to send this letter right away, I will limit myself to wishing you all the best. I will write separately in a few days. I am hugging and kissing you tenderly.*

> *Loving you,*
> *Dora*

In all of these letters what is concealed is often more important than what is revealed. The war began on September 1, 1939. My grandmother writes that she has not heard from any member of the family for nine months, that is, since January 1940. She also suggests that money should not be sent but does not give the reason. Because mail was read, money would certainly be confiscated.

For the same reason avoiding censorship she does not allude to the horrors of the past nine months moving from one apartment to the next, the tormenting of Jews in the streets during the first few months after the war began, the wearing of yellow arm bands, the curfews that prevented freedom of movement, and the final march to the Lodz Ghetto with her one allowed suitcase. In reading, I had to continuously remind myself that her correspondents know nothing of the terrible hardships of her situation. These she must hide, first because of the censors, and second because she doesn't want to upset her "children" [my grandmother always referred to my parents as her "children"].

Her main source of both mail and a promise of provisions is through her brother-in-law Henri. Henri and his wife Tania were Communists and left Poland before the war for Riga in the Soviet Union. Because of the secret treaty signed by Hitler and Stalin in August 1939, correspondence with family members in the Soviet Union was possible until June 1941 when the Germans invaded Russia.

No matter how horrible the situation, my grandmother hopes that the war will end soon, and that she will see her children again. Certainly, none could imagine the horrors of Nazi policies toward Jews. And my grandmother, who graduated from a German Gymnasium, became fluent in German, loves German literature, and reads Heine and Schiller cannot imagine the nature of this war. She tries hard to express optimism about the end of the war. She is also clearly annoyed with my father, from whom she has not received a letter, and, as was characteristic of her, honest when she feels neglected. She lets him know her disappointment.

For the recipients of her letters, the lack of understanding of her circumstances cannot be bridged. My grandmother has to conceal the details of her confinement because of German censorship. She maintains a delicate balance, wanting to spare her children and relatives from the conditions in which she lives, and of course wanting to avoid confiscation of her postcards. She is always the "responsible" mother or niece, interested in her family's well-being, and in the beginning conceals the conditions of her existence. However, as conditions in the ghetto became worse—above all the lack of food—she tries to communicate her desperate need for provisions. Hunger is the most consistent theme of life in the ghetto—relentless hunger followed by disease and death.

On the same day that my grandmother writes to my parents and her brother, she also writes in Russian to her Uncle Julius Love and her Aunt Ida, who arranged for my parents' visa to the U.S. Uncle Love, who lived in Poland when it was under Russian rule, does not know Polish, or certainly is not fluent in it. My grandmother therefore writes to him in Russian. In the letter she thanks both her aunt and uncle profusely for their assistance and for bringing her children to the United States.

May 23, 1940

My dearly beloved Uncle and Aunt, if anybody can beg God for your health, and long life, it's me! I never forget that you are the most dear, most beloved Uncle, who is so good to my dearest children. Thanks to you they are happy, they work, and they are healthy.

I ask of fate only that I can see you and my dear Auntie, and personally thank you for all the good you do for me and for my children who love you so. If they can only repay you for all the good you showed us. I shake your hand and kiss you tenderly.

Sincerely and devoted to you,
Mania

Julius Love was prescient and thoughtful in bringing my parents to the U.S., thus saving their lives. He provided a room and initially carfare so they could get to and from work. By this time, they had already left my uncle's home and established their own practice in a Polish neighborhood in Philadelphia.

After my father passed his Boards following a one-year internship at Roxborough Memorial Hospital, he was able to set up his own practice. He asked for a loan from Uncle Love of $300 to rent a house and open his office, which Uncle Love granted with interest. According to my parents, they left Uncle Love on good terms; certainly they deeply appreciated how important he had been in their lives. He died shortly after I was born in 1942 and did not leave my parents any of his estate. My parents were always proud of their independent start. They never regretted it.

In 1940, postal communication "between the ghetto world was continually disrupted by the German restrictions which led in certain periods to a total postal embargo."[15] Between July 17, 1940, and September 16, 1940, "postal communication with the outside world halted with the exception of telegrams and registered letters."[16]

The next three postcards are numbered and appear to have been written on the same date, September 26, 1940.

> *September 26, 1940*
>
> *Postcard 1*
>
> *My beloved Children, Aunt and Uncle,*
>
> *We finally have an opportunity to write a few lines to you. We are also looking forward to receiving a letter from you. I frequently get cards from Halinochka, my only treasure. Mikhal annoys me immensely though, he writes close to nothing. What could be the reason? Are you that busy my child? Dear Uncle and Aunt also keep silent. I receive not a word from them. I hope they are healthy.*
>
> *I would so very much like to hear good news from you. I especially wonder about our dearest Rudek; what is going on with him? He used to always be so regular with his letters; now throughout the entire war, he has hardly even written a word to me. My dear brother never once wrote to me in these hard times. This matter makes me very uneasy. God forbid anything bad happened! My God this hard war has separated us all and now we can't even communicate in writing.*

Postcard 2

We ask you not to forget to write. There are lucky families, mothers and parents who receive more detailed news from America. My heart aches so, my longing is so profound. Dear children, my sunshine, Halus, how are all of you-are you cheerful and healthy? You are my only comfort in this hard life.

I am healthy. We live together: I, Dora, Abram, and his brothers. I have no idea where Papa's brother currently lives.[17] *Possibly he is with Fredzio* [another brother] *in Krzemieniec. I wrote to them but no response. My dear children, we received three packages from Riga. I can't figure out if they were sent directly from Henri or from the organization in Riga.*[18] *Henri doesn't write to me at all. In any case, I send my sincerest thanks to you for the package. Because of it we were able to have good ourishment for a while.*

Postcard 3

Dear Children, Uncle and Aunt!

You most likely received by now two of the cards written earlier today as well as two cards written in the past week.[19]

You know everything about us. Please send us fats more often: Provence oil [possibly referring to olive oil]; *butter, cheese, milk, smoked fish, kosher sausage, canned goods, sardines, oil, cofiee, cocoa, chocolate and so on. We can't get any of it. Also we can't get soap or Nivea cream. In case you plan to arrange it through an organization — these are the main products.*

Let God end this harsh war soon! We are so tired. Write to us more often about everything. Hala everybody reads your letters. Please don't forget to write to Abram and Aunt. Please write to Adzio [a nickname for Arkadius, the, son of Dora and Abram]. *They are better ofi in Warsaw.*

I kiss you and bless you from the bottom of my heart. I miss you terribly, Mommy

Aunt and Uncle send their greetings as well.

By the fall of 1940, the food situation was desperate. Indeed, by August 1940, a month before these letters were written, 70 percent of the ghetto inhabitants had no more money. By September, a public support system was implemented for those who did not have resources to purchase food — about 100,000 of a total population of 166,000. Those on welfare (i.e., not employed) were also exempt from paying rent, and cheap meals could be obtained at community or building kitchens.

David Horowitz describes the Germans' governing economic strategy:

> The Jews of the ghetto would work, they would produce, and they would yield up the remainder of their portable wealth. Gold, silver, crystal, furs, cottons, woolens, everything worth acquiring or refurbishing was collected, stored, and then sold to provide for their upkeep. The Jews would be made to give and give, and the Germans would take from the ghetto whatever could be made or remade in ghetto workshops, then collected, warehoused, and sold.[20]

During the fall of 1940, the period in which my grandmother's postcards were written, the Germans set up a residential food distribution system. This was a reaction to the price manipulation in ghetto stores. Ration coupons were distributed to each person, and the ghetto administration kept a file of each person's name. They could use their ration card only at a designated grocery or at bread and milk distribution centers. The actual distribution of these cards took place in December 1940, several months after the above postcards were written.

The standard used for food distribution by the Germans was that it should be equivalent to what German prisoners received, suggesting concretely how ghetto residents were viewed—as equivalent to criminals. Isaiah Trunk writes, "Food items such as vegetables or groceries were on a starvation level throughout the ghetto's existence; meat and fats were seldom distributed." He notes that "Neither the dysentery epidemic of 1940, nor typhus and typhoid fever in the subsequent years, caused the high mortality in the ghetto. The angel of death of the Lodz Ghetto was hunger. The results of the enduring, unceasing hunger became simply catastrophic, for the health condition of the ghetto population...."[21]

Oskar Rosenfeld, a journalist and playwright, who was deported from Vienna to the Lodz Ghetto in the winter of 1942, writes in his notebooks about a period 15 months later than my grandmother's letters; however, the food shortages in the period that both she and he lived through were similar.

> About "hunger." "We don't talk about eating" one of the many famished women said once. Such a conversation stimulates the stomach, gives off secretions, thereby weakening the organism. It happened frequently that people who talked themselves into the

illusion that they were eating foods from which they had long abstained displayed severe nervous disorders and turned outright wild during the night. We tell each other stories about clothing one evening, another time about travels, then again we talk about the books we once read... We also avoid any kind of physical exertion. Every step must be weighed.... Otherwise one gets tired very easily.[22]

He describes the soup that is distributed in community kitchens:

About 200,000 portions of soup were dispensed daily in the ghetto. What *a* wonderful word is "soup"! Here it was a curse for no prison inmate would be satisfied with such contemptible stuff.... Carrots, water beets, red beets, a few kernels of barley swimming around in the warm water—that was called soup. This caricature of soup was the major cause of the hunger symptoms, the famine edema that became matter-of-fact in the ghetto rather than a phenomenon. People were drinking, eating, slurping, gobbling the soup, brutally suppressing thereby with it the subjectively unpleasant feeling of hunger. The stomach was full for a short while. The main goal of nutrition, the essential character of nutrition: the ingestion of valuable elements was not serviced by it.[23]

Although this description of the pervasive hunger can't be expressed in my grandmother's letters, this is what it looks and feels like. My grandmother is lucky in that some packages arrive and sustain the family for a short time, but the German authorities frequently do not allow packages to get through at all, and for long periods, the population faces the kind of hunger that Rosenfeld describes.

My grandmother is not aware of the extent to which the mail was either not sent or not distributed. She expresses her anger and pain of abandonment by those dearest and closest to her. Finally she expresses what hope still remains for her—a hope that perhaps sustained her as long as it did
—that God could not allow such an atrocity to continue.

October 1, 1940

My Dearest Uncle, Aunt and Children,

I write to you very often. Last week I wrote two letters. I do not get any news from you. There is quite a long silence from Halinochka. It makes me so uneasy. My entire body hurts. I ask you to write more often. And from Dear Jakob [her brother] I receive not a single word.

How are you all doing and why aren't you writing? How is anyone supposed to be strong enough to withstand the ups and downs of life. There could be so much to communicate through the many months of this evil war. I have to separate myself from the overflow of feelings and ask only for the ones that are most beautiful. Live and remain strong to survive. Tomorrow is the new year. I wish you happiness and many blessings.

I kiss you, Mommy

Dora and Abram send their heartfelt greetings.

My grandmother expresses her frustration with her children for not writing. But she censors herself by not allowing her feelings of desertion, sadness, and anger to overwhelm her. Rather she chooses to stay with "what is most beautiful" and hopeful: "live and remain strong to survive." Certainly the meaning of Rosh Hashanah and Yom Kippur when Jews are commanded to ask forgiveness of those whom they have wronged has deep meaning for her in this time of despair and suffering. She concludes with wishes for Rosh Hashanah, which at this point the ghetto administration still allow the inhabitants to celebrate by taking a leave from their workplaces.

In the following letter, addressed to her brother in Chicago, my grandmother is trying to understand why my parents would leave their Uncle Love and move out to set up their own practice.

October 8, 1940

My good, dear Rudek,

In my previous card I asked you a lot about the children. I would like you to write me very exactly what happened. What was also planned and discussed is that Uncle would turn over his ofiice, practice and apartment to Mikhal. Is he perhaps unhappy with the children? Why? I worry a lot that the children are looking for an apartment and they don't live with Uncle. I am very curious and uneasy about it. He should help the children and be a good uncle to them, and now in the end they have to leave his house.

I am ashamed for people over here. They are already buzzing and thinking unpleasant thoughts. Do the children have enough to live on? Do they make money?

Hala asks me about sending clothes. I am very much in need of garments,
warm garments. I grew very sensitive to the cold. Night clothes, bed clothes,
a robe, stockings, dresses, a coat but how can I expand your budget. When
would uncle be willing to send it to me?

We have Yom Kippur. Be happy and healthy for many good years. Please
write about everything soon.

Yours,
Maria, Dora and Abram

My grandmother reveals how anxious she is about her children's future. Since they do not want to trouble her she has no context to understand how they "up and leave him" when Uncle Love was offering his practice and *a* place to live. She alludes to her shame before her relatives that the amazing "deal her children had" of being cared for by a wealthy uncle is not the reality.

It is significant that as soon as my parents moved out of Uncle Love's home, they changed their name from Love, which was a condition of Uncle Love's bringing them to the States and becoming his heirs, back to Wolkowicz. And of course in making this move they renounced any claim to inheriting his wealth.

I understand why they would not want to explain all of this to my grandmother, and yet the lack of explanation caused my grandmother grief and pain. She could not understand the circumstances that determined their decision nor the professional opportunities that existed for them by leaving Uncle Love. It must have aggravated her already horrific life to think that her children were not honest with her and might have made a terrible decision.

In the same letter, my grandmother alludes to the other great distress of her life: she has no warm clothes. The winter of 1940-41 was among the coldest on record. To keep warm, people burned their furniture. My grandmother, like all ghetto residents, was allowed to leave with one suitcase that she could carry, and now she finds she cannot clothe herself properly in the bitter cold. And like many of the other residents, she has no goods of value that she could exchange for either food or clothing.

My grandmother now writes to my parents at their new address, 3061 Richmond Street, located in northeast Philadelphia, a Polish working class neighborhood, where they have established their residence and opened an office in order to begin their medical practice. The postcards are now using the name Wolkowicz for the return address. All previous letters were addressed using the name Love.

October 10, 1940

No. 1

My Dearest Children,

Yesterday, I received your dear letter. I was looking forward to getting it for so long. My dear Mikhal, you finally wrote a few words to your mother! I wasn't really able to explain your silence because I didn't have any reason to complain so far. You always wrote regularly. I very much regret that Uncle and Aunt don't seem to be able to write even a few words to us. After all staying in touch with us brings us our greatest pleasure.

My Halus! My only sunshine and solace in life. I thank you for your detailed letter, for your efforts of tenderness toward me. On many topics you seem to be sparing with information and you don't explain how you got your professional training [most likely, secretarial courses]. *Most of all, I am surprised and grieved that you departed from the house of your good and devoted Uncle.*

No. 2

What is it children, what is happening? I have asked so many times already. How did you make Uncle angry? Abram and others keep asking questions and the entire story is very awkward for me. And just like any one would, it gave me great satisfaction that you were getting along with Uncle so well! But never mind. Germans say, "Happy is the one who forgets what he is unable to change."

Please my sunshine, write something extra in a little letter, which is included in a regular letter, just for me. Tell me exactly what happened.

I think that I am occasionally becoming a burden to you… but I am completely without means. It is hard to live on charity, even sister's charity. I feel that they [Dora and Abram] *guard their money, now.*[24]

No. 3

I am sending the third card now because we don't dare to write letters. Can one really share everything that concerns the heart? But that is how it is. We are healthy. We live together. Please Hala don't send packages to me, but to all of us. We are together, but I have no money.

We received three packages with food but I am not sure whether they came directly from America or whether they came from Henri. For us it a delightful support (a lot of various fats, cheese, cocoa, flour, butter). Now I have asked Henri to send us something salted and smoked, lots of Provence oil, kosher meats, by all means milk, canned goods, chocolate, soap, lotion and so on. I thank you many fold for remembering us.

Yesterday, I went to the cemetery and Papa should try his best for us. Amen.

For Yom Kippur I wish you a happy year, many blessings in all aspects of your life. May you always be happy and content together. Amen. Don't forget to write. I shed tears of longing.

Your loving mother

No. 4

In any case, my dear children, I congratulate you, my beautiful doctor in America! Let the powerful God hear my prayer and may happiness and contentment never abandon you! Our blessed Papa, who loved his children so, also cares. Please write to me exactly about everything, about how you started your new life.

All of Papa's brothers are in Warsaw now. Quite unexpectedly I received a letter from Warsaw from Artek. He loves me very much or so he writes. After he received my reply he was questioning me a lot about all the brothers. They are likely doing very poorly.

It is clear from my grandmother's letters that living together in two rooms with her relatives has become extremely difficult. She feels, as she did after my grandfather died, that she is viewed as a "burden." She also knows that if she did not have support from the outside, she would be completely beholden to her sister and brother-in-law.

As in the previous letter, my grandmother expresses her distress to my parents that the "grand plan" of inheriting Uncle Love's practice and living in his home has fallen by the wayside. She cannot imagine why my parents sought their own independence or that it would work out if they did. She is ashamed in front of her sister and others that her children were seemingly "expelled from paradise." Their survival without Uncle Love's help is beyond what she can imagine.

From this point on, my grandmother's letters are frantic. She repeats herself because she doesn't know if her letters have been received. But it is clear that despite her statement that she is healthy, she is not, and she is totally dependent on her sister and brother-in-law for support.

I cite several passages from these letters in which she expresses greater and greater fear and desperation regarding her survival, and anguish that her children have forsaken her.

November 11, 1940

My Dearest Children,

I wrote many letters to you, but I receive very few in return. It has been five weeks since I got a postcard from you and it was very brief, as if you have nothing to share with me. I have many friends who receive many letters from America; they also get money and packages with food. You are forgetting my sunshine that I am just a poor widow. I hope to hear good news from you- that is what keeps me alive. You totally forgot about me. It doesn't seem to be Uncle and Aunt's style either [to write letters].

We live together. I don't want to be a burden to you. People don't have enough for themselves my child [she is referring to her sister and her family]. You have one mother, a widow. I shouldn't be tortured. I am completely without means. No packages. I don't want strangers to be supporting me when my child could still be willing to help me. Don't send me any goods [by this she means clothes]. I cannot pay the customs. I have no money.

Mikhal's parents are doing well and they are receiving your letters and packages.

Mother

It is painful for me to read this postcard. Surely my parents must have been sending packages.[25] But my grandmother does not receive them. German officials often confiscated packages and the mail was always erratic. My grandmother, however, interprets the lack of response as neglect and abandonment. When I reflect on why my parents never told me about her postcards, I believe that this is the heart of the matter: they may not have understood the desperate situation in which my grandmother's found herself until after the war ended and the truth about the conditions in the ghetto were revealed. My grandmother died not knowing that they tried.

My parents' inability to even imagine the extreme deprivation of everything that makes life bearable sufficient food and shelter, work, close relationships with friends and family is understandable. When the war ended and they understood the reality of my grandmother's life in the ghetto, they were traumatized by the knowledge. One expression of their trauma was that they never talked about how my grandmother died. It was implicitly off limits, so while growing up, I never asked. Until I found the letters I didn't know the circumstances of my grandmother's final years.

Four days after her despairing postcard, my grandmother writes about the importance of remembering my grandfather.

November 15, 1940

My Dearest Children,

I have already written five cards to you this month. The main thing I want to write and remind you about is the anniversary of blessed Papa, which according to Jewish tradition falls on December 11. That means on the eleventh day of Kislev. My dearest sunshine, at least for one hour on this day, at the time when you receive this letter, remember and think peacefully about our beloved Papa. I will certainly be by his grave, adorning it with flowers.[26] He liked quiet gentleness, the good Sasha!

Artek wrote a letter to me yesterday. He complains that he doesn't get any letters from you. You wrote that he confirmed receiving a package. I already asked him five times to send the address of Tania and Nunia,[27] but he doesn't answer. We can get beautiful healthy packages from Moscow here up to ten kilograms. Starting with hard cured fish, fats, chocolate and so on. Perhaps he will still answer his sister in law.

I heartily kiss you, your loving and longing Mother

The next postcard acknowledges receipt of my parents' packages, although they had arrived four months earlier. She also mentions that her sister Dora is now managing a community kitchen where people go to have meals.

November 18ᵗʰ, 1940

On the 17ᵗʰ of November, I already wrote you two cards. What can you discuss with your loved ones on such a short page. This and that and nothing really fully. Hala you wrote that you had sent me packages and money. Three or four months ago we received three packages. I shared the food with others. I don't need much. Dora luckily got a position as a manager of the community kitchen, where we get tickets for dinner. Each of us gets one except Abram. I unfortunately am an unpaid manager in the house in our neighborhood. I have a lot of work and frustration. Now I can see that I am quite strong in the fields of economy and being helpful. People often wonder and are entranced by my creations in cooking. Sometimes I am very proud of myself.[28]

On the 20th of November, my grandmother writes a desperate and angry card, berating Uncle Love for not helping her.

Life teaches us to take better care of ourselves. The softer you are in life, the more you are punished by fate. But this is how it is. Yesterday I asked Uncle Love what was the reason that he let my children move out, and I asked him to help you with your house. I also gave him a "mouthful." God help you without him.

I would like him to support me. I am totally without any means. This matter makes my life very difficult. I will even turn for support to our president [she means Rumkovski] *until I receive something from you. What's more I haven't heard a word from Rudek for the past fifteen months of this war. The lack of letters makes me nervous… until I receive letters in his own hand I won't calm down. He is always so good to me and is always on time. Is he by any chance sick! Halus, please write me the truth.*

I kiss you from the bottom of my heart,
Mommy

My grandmother is starving, desperate that she cannot support herself, and dependent on the "kindness" of her sister and brother-in-law for her survival. According to her previous correspondence before the war, this relationship was always fraught with tension and in the desperate situation of their lives in the ghetto has become even more so. She also fears that something has happened to her brother since she has not heard from him in fifteen months. Her anger with Uncle Love comes through clearly in this letter. She feels betrayed that she pinned her hopes on the love and support that he promised to her children. Her letters become more distressed and frantic from this time on. It is becoming clear that the war is not ending and that she has no means to support herself. It seems more and more likely that she will never see her children again.

On the same day, November 20, Abram writes to my parents congratulating them on, as he puts it, their "new firm" in reality a three-room doctor's office on the ground floor of a rented house in a working class neighborhood.

Dear Children!

I read with pleasure your two letters. I am very glad that Mikhal is independent now and that he has started his own firm. I congratulate you and wish you much luck and happiness. We, thank God, are all healthy and we are living all together: myself, Dora and my brothers, Sasha and Boris. Please write to your mother and tell her to eat more because she is so thin. Dora works in the kitchen 14 hours a day. We weren't fortunate to find employment. Stay healthy my dear children. I kiss you and greet you from the bottom of my heart.

Yours, Abram

Aunt Dora sends her kisses and greetings.

I have mulled over this postcard many times. First because I needed to understand that my grandmother's description of the relationships among family members reflects her despair at being dependent on others for support. However, at this point, her sister, who is older than she, is working in a community kitchen 14 hours a day her meager wage supporting everyone.

To put this in context, in July 1940, of 13,395 women in the ghetto between the ages of 46 and 60, only a very small percentage were working. Most of the women in this age range were listed as "without occupation" before entering the ghetto. This did not mean they did not work but that they did not fit the occupations used by the Germans to categorize them. Dora did in fact have a recognizable occupation. She ran the pension that she and her husband owned for many years and therefore, unlike my grandmother, she was qualified for the position in the community kitchen. This suggests more complicated relationships and dependencies than my grandmother reveals. The hours that Abram reports are shocking, especially when one considers that it was ghetto residents, not the Germans, who organized the workplace.

I am also puzzled about Abram's concern about my grandmother's health. Is he reporting something beyond the lack of food: perhaps her psychological state that is so distraught she "cannot eat," or more likely her attempt to not eat much of the food in the house because of her concern about being dependent on others. In all of my grandmother's postcards, she emphasizes that whatever is sent is shared with everyone and that my parents must be mindful of this.

Two postcards dated December 9 and 24, 1940, again reflect my grandmother's need for food, her feeling of being deserted, and perhaps being treated worse than other members of the family in Warsaw.

My dearest children,

I am writing many postcards to you, three or four a week. I am sorry that you might not be getting my postcards. I have with many thanks received your postcards through the Red Cross, and I answered them. I repeat myself so frequently because I am not sure you have my letters in your possession.

Artek received your package two months ago, and so did Mikhal's parents. Why my children have you forgotten about me. I have written many times to Artek. He should send me the addresses of Tania, Nunia, and Pepa. Here in the Ghetto, people receive many packages from Russia-10 to 15 kilograms with all good things- cocoa, fats, flour, milk, butter, cheese, canned goods, smoked fish, ham, zwiebak.

This is how you look when you are dying and are a forlorn widow, who is most of all forgotten. Jakob's silence makes me so sad. Please write me the truth.

I kiss you from the bottom of my heart full of longing. Mother

Letters from February to June 1941

The first letter of 1941 is desperate and angry. In addition to undergoing the harsh, cold winter of 1940-41, my grandmother is angered by relatives who gossip that her children who went to America have been rejected by Uncle Love. She writes, "Her evil look was enough for me. I don't like it that people here are starting to think that you are doing poorly." To understand these sentiments, it is necessary to know that my parents' being able to go to the States and under what seemed like such generous terms—a place to live and a chance to inherit a medical practice— was viewed with both awe and envy by family members. I think my grandmother's only pleasure at this point was in their having been saved and so generously. In her eyes, there seems to be an unfriendly gloating: "so it is not as she [my grandmother] described for her children in America." In this letter my grandmother uses the Polish phrase "zlamane koryoto" literally "broken trough" to describe what she now understands my parents' life in the States to be. But more importantly for her, it means that by leaving Uncle Love, her children no longer have the means to help her out.

February, 25, 1941 My Dearest Children!

I haven't written to you for three weeks already. And in fact, in seven weeks, I didn't get a card from you. You should stay healthy and happy- this is all that I strive for in life and it needs to be enough for me. Yesterday, I had a happy day. I got such a warm and darling letter from dear Jakob. Thank God he is healthy and cheerful. He sent me a package with food. Unfortunately, I haven't received it yet, but his care for me brought tears to my eyes. My good boy![29] *How he loves you! He always writes about you in his letters to me. He says that you are doing well. Mikhal works well and has a beautiful practice, and what is most important, Uncle Love is on friendly terms with you. I want to believe all his beautiful stories. But you children, Mischa* [another nick name for my father] *works so hard and you had to borrow money and so on. It is difficult for me to have courage. People already have "vengeful tongues" and it is bad for me in my situation, being without any means. It sounded good that my daughter was a "millionaire" and help will come.*[30]

How are you my children. Keep your business ties with Uncle Love. I don't want you to break this thread. Uncle did so much for us. I love him very much. We here are all well. Aunt A is very weak and she needs to be taken care of. Mischa, please advise me: my eyesight is failing. What should I do? You have to have "an invitation" for me to America.[31] *Please most of all write. I kiss you, your always loving Mother.*

Upon arriving in the U.S., my parents immediately established close ties with my grandmother's brother Rudek, whose real name was Jakob Kagan, later renamed by immigration officials John Kanne, a name he kept. At the time of this letter, he was by then an established lawyer in Chicago. He and my parents were always close and he visited us twice a year. He was a man of great charm, athletic, with a strong body that he worked hard to keep in shape, a singer with an operatic voice (he auditioned unsuccessfully for the Chicago Opera Company). He had an important male friend with whom he vacationed. As an adult I realized he was probably gay. He and my mother were always close, and when he visited he was the focus of her attention

In a letter to her brother, my grandmother shares with him her anger at my parents; apparently they have written that they don't have means to support her until they have paid off their debts.

March 10, 1941

My dearly beloved brother,

You have certainly received my many letters. It is important for me to know if you received my important letter from February 27. On the same day I also wrote to my children and I am very curious if they have received my letter. They should answer to me promptly. I also received this week a detailed letter from Hala via air mail. The children write that they are doing well, the practice developing nicely, and they are on best of terms with uncle, who loves them very much. Unfortunately, they have debt in connection with their apartment but they are paying it off. Mischa remarked that when they going to have more money he would help everyone more. They don't have the means yet. Their mother, the wretched widow, should think how not to become a burden in her last days. It is expressed quite cynically so cold and without concern for me! It hurts me so. I was looking forward to so much love from Hala! In the meantime, he informs me that he sends aid packages to his parents every month, whereas for me no support. I haven't seen a single package for ten months from my only beloved daughter. I the poor widow. And on whom should she want me to depend for my sustenance? Aunt is also weak. She has to be fed.

My only daughter. Laughable, her husband writes that I must hang on for support, the times will get better and what should I do now. Uncle Love must be on Hala's side! He doesn't even write anymore. We thought more of our parents. Mischa's parents have it very, very good! I would wish it to myself! After all, Hala doesn't forget to send them a package every month. In February, after ten months, I received a meager, little package. I am ashamed in front of my friends! This is my life! To be a burden to people who do not want me, and who do not love me. My dear brother, I turn to you. Hala forgot about me. She doesn't love her mother anymore. [The last sentence is illegible.]

This heartbreaking letter suggests another reason why my parents never shared this correspondence with me. It is very possible that their understanding of the situation was limited. No one could envision the situation of the Lodz or Warsaw Ghettos. The information was not yet available. Once my parents knew the truth, this letter must have caused pain and guilt. And in her desperation my grandmother did not blame the Nazis for stealing packages, and for her misery or at least not in censored letters. Ultimately what hurt her most was the seeming neglect of her needs and what appeared to be my parents' indifference.

Writing only four days later, with the tone used with her children, she shows the face of the caring mother. The other face, her anger and disappointment with her children, she shows only to her brother.

March 14, 1941

My Dearest Children,

You have surely received my many letters. It is the fourth card this month. Today, I am writing on the birthday of my child. This is the only way I could send you my congratulations and my warmest wishes and blessings.[32] *Soon afterwards comes the 15th of May, Mischa's birthday. I combine both of the festive days, which I love so much into one joy and send you my best wishes and blessings. May your home always be full of joy and blessings. May you always be happy and joyful together until a ripe old age. May I see you once again, may your happiness comfort me, and may I experience beautiful moments with you. May you bring beauty into your home and enjoy it. This is what I wish for you. It suffices to pour my overflow of feelings on paper. On this day I dress my thoughts in flowers and birthday cakes. Be joyful and happy, and blessed by our mother.*

Do you prefer someone else over me. My deepest feelings are not returned by you. I would like to be together with you in America. You should provide me with an invitation. I can do nothing here! Are you in touch with my dear Jakob? Why does he visit you so little [my grandmother does not realize that they are a two-day expensive train trip apart]. *I wish he kept closer with you. He is so loving and so good to us. He always writes to me about you. How is Uncle Love? Are you in close contact with him? I love him so much and I wish you had warm feelings for him too.*

I cordially greet you and kiss you from the bottom of my heart. Your mother

I read this letter with a mother's heart. Being in such a dire situation, she is hurt by her children's apparent neglect, which is incomprehensible and so painful for her. The sentence "do you prefer someone else over me" expresses her desperation and anger. In addition, she still believes that they could rescue her and bring her to them.

The Litzmannstadt ghetto, March 22, 1941

My Dearest Children!

I constantly write to you and hope that dear God will help you receive my letters. This way you could at least partly receive news about me. This month I thankfully confirm receiving your numerous and detailed letters [that she had not seen previously]. *I am so happy that you are doing well my children. You should only strive for the good in your life. Your house should forever be filled with happiness and blessings as well as with flowers and joy. But you shouldn't forget about your mother, the widow. She should be provided for by her daughter with the necessary support and aid. Before the war had started I was provided with timely support. Now you let me down to depend on other people. This is beyond my comprehension and my disposition. My blood grows cold and bread doesn't bring me nourishment. I depend only on my children (when fate laughed at me like it has) and my only brother, who is always thinking about me. My eyes are weak and I am in need of good care. Aunt is also very ill. You need to get me to America. I cannot do anything here under such circumstances. Yesterday Mikhal's aunt P[33] was here. She had a present and demanded the return of a striped table cloth. She is shocked that you don't send her any packages. She is an insane person! How I would like to spend my last years together with you and see your happiness. Aunt Dora had no letters* [from you], *Abram and I neither. The brothers of Abram also didn't.*

I kiss you warmly. I miss you in my heart, Mom.

From week to week the letters become more desperate and the anger and despair at her children's seeming neglect more emphatic. On April 10, 1941, my grandmother again writes to her brother about her children's neglect of her and care of my father's parents in Warsaw. It is also the angriest letter of all regarding her sister and brother-in law. She writes, "*I am quite fed up with both of them, as you yourself observed when you stayed with us in Lodz* [she is clearly referring to a visit before the war began].

The last two letters that my grandmother ever wrote to my parents are filled with loving sentiments.

On April 22, 1941, my mother's birthday, she writes:

Today is the happiest birthday of my only beloved daughter. I spent the moment silently and quite lonely though ordinarily it is festive and full of flowers. Today everyone lives for himself. I haven't given thought for a long time about the day I gave birth to you, about the world that seemed so beautiful and full of hopes of how we would bring you up, our beautiful and darling child. To be a reliable and a good person, and to be a good wife. And the birth was so dangerous for me that I could have just remained a memory.

Why did I live so many years to be tortured now. No parents and friends have saved me.

But I live and I would like to experience your happiness. Is my life worth living. My imagination worked so hard today and throughout the night. My child today you turn 32. May God let you live with your wonder ful husband to a ripe old age. Dear Mischa will turn 32 on May 16.[34] You should always be content and happy. You should experience joy and happiness in your life. Today's day is hard for me. I miss you my dear children with my whole heart. Why don't you prepare papers for me? Artek wouldn't let me know what I should prepare for the journey.[35]

I kiss you. Mother

Again, in the next letter written on June 12, 1941, and the last one my parents would ever receive from her, she expresses her gratitude for a package finally received, however entirely as she says "pulverized." She also instructs them on the most reliable way to send packages through an agency in New York the lettering is illegible since they indicate they have sent many more packages.

Clearly, she now realizes that my parents have been sending packages and she acknowledges this and thanks them. It appears that she has shared this letter with her sister and brother-in-law so speaks of "we" in the first paragraph and then speaks of herself in the third person as "Mania." In the last paragraph she speaks again of "we" wanting to see how my parents are living.

Children you write that you had sent many others and we are waiting for them. I implore you and the dear uncle to write to Tania and the siblings, so that they send us aid immediately.

Henri, the bad boy, doesn't answer any of my letters. All the aid goes fast and is very good. We don't get packages from Tania and Henri. Write to them immediately. It was so nice to have had butter in the past year. Henri and Hala should send us packages. Mania [what my grandmother was usually called] *asks for them very much.*

Otherwise all is the same. I would like to enjoy the last years of my life together with you. Your success and your wonderful life make me happy.

We would very much like to see your house and your lovely living room. Provided you can afiord it, it is better to have less but the only the best.

May God always give you happiness, joy, love, and satisfaction with each other. My little Hala, how are you. [The next sentence is unclear but seems to ask if my mother does not plan to have a child yet.]

We didn't go to the cemetery to visit Papa for a long time because I had joint inflammation in my hands and feet. Now I am better and had a memorable visit. How is your relationship with Uncle? My wish is that you live and are respected.

Uncle doesn't write me, nor does Artek.

Kisses from your mom

Dora and Abram send their greetings to you.

My grandmother survived for another 17 months. Her hope that she would see her children one day sustained her. When I visited the Lodz Archives in 2012, I received documents that included my grandmother's death certificate, indicating the cause of death on September 28, 1942, as "malnutrition." The efficiency of the Nazis prescribed that every death of "natural causes" be recorded by the Jewish doctors who were in charge of the clinics and hospitals in the Lodz Ghetto. The indecipherable signature of the attending physician on the death certificate was that of a Jewish doctor.

My grandmother was 58 when she died, too young for the horrific transport of elderly people and children that took place in the first six days of September 1942. This was 20 days after the deportation of all adults over 65, and 15,859 children under 10 years old. This event, known as the "Sperre" [literally, a ban on walking in the street][36] was the last major deportation before the Lodz Ghetto was liquidated in August 1944.[37] By then the population had been reduced from 163,000 inhabitants to 44,000. Virtually all of the remaining population, primarily adults of working age, were sent to Auschwitz and died there. In all, only 844 souls of the original 163,000 survived.

By September 1942, the inhabitants of the Lodz Ghetto knew that their children and elders would meet certain death when rounded up. By this time, the Germans were only interested in preserving the lives of working adults and children who were old enough to be taught a trade. Rumkovski knew their fate, but in his speech before the round-ups began tried to justify his cooperation with the Nazis by emphasizing that he could thereby save those who would remain.

This was shortly after Czerniakow, the head of the Warsaw Ghetto, committed suicide in July rather than submit to German orders to transport children and older people.

Rumkovksi also knew what was to come. In his speech on September 4, 1942, he said that failure to comply with the decree would compel the Germans to do it. "But we have decided to do it ourselves because we do not want and are unable to transform it into a horrific, terrible disaster."[38] He acknowledged that 20,000 elderly people over the age of 65 and children under 10 would be taken. To those who assembled to hear his speech, he said, "I bear no tidings of consolation today. Neither have I come to calm you today, but rather to expose all of your pain and sorrow. I have come like a thief to deprive you of that which is dearest to your heart." He told his audience that he had succeeded in having the number to be deported dropped from 24,000 to 20,000.

Arnold Mostowicz, a Lodz doctor who wrote his memoir late in life, describes his own cowardice with shame in an interview in the documentary film *Fotoamator* (1998), directed by Dariusz Jablonski:

> When Rumkowski learned that the Germans had decided to remove all the sick, the elderly, and the children, he called a meeting of doctors.... I took part in that meeting. In the course of it ninety percent of the doctors agreed that it had to be done, that the decision must be observed. At the same time they were fully aware that to those deported it meant death. Naturally, you can ask me—and it would be a fair question—how did I react? Well I reacted in the most cowardly way imaginable: I said nothing. I cannot tell you what made me act that way, except on things which I am sure of now.... Personally, I was under no threat; that was one of the reasons for my silence, but it would be too easy to say that it was the only reason. I guess I kept quiet because I was ashamed to say that we should do as the Germans told us, since there was no escape from their decision, but at the same time to admit that it was an utter disgrace.[39]

Beginning on Friday, September 5, 1942, the round-up began by the Jewish Police and what was known as the White Guard, ghetto porters and teamsters known for their strength. Their job: the horrific work of tearing children from their parents, and forcing the elderly and sick into waiting wagons. For their labor, their own children and elders would be saved. By the next day, September 6, the Germans decided that the Jews could not do this job satisfactorily so they initiated a rampage of sadistic cruelty—children shot for fun, older people dragged into the carts—a nightmare that few could have imagined—their worst fears of Gehenna[40] realized. An estimated 15,859 persons were deported and approximately 600 were shot on the spot.

I do not know why my grandmother died shortly after this horrific deportation. I want to believe that she chose the timing of her death. She gave way to starvation because at this point there were no signs of the war ending, and the idea of her ever seeing her children again seemed impossible. There was nothing to live for. If indeed this was a choice on her part, it saved her from a more terrible death in Auschwitz.

A comforting thought for me is that my grandmother was buried in the Lodz Cemetery in what is now a huge grassy meadow. In the first years of the ghetto simple markers with names and dates of birth and death were placed on the graves; however, by the time of my grandmother's death those who died were so numerous that they were quickly disposed of and buried in nameless plots.

When I visited the Lodz Cemetery in 2012, it was a rambling and beautiful old forest with crumbling tombstones surrounded by overgrown grass and weeds. I was moved by the fact that my grandmother and my grandfather were buried not only in the same cemetery, but in *close* proximity. My grandfather's gravesite was not far from the huge grassy field, and although his gravestone was desecrated by vandals, I knew it was his since he was buried next to his parents, their names clearly displayed on their tombstones. I comfort myself that finally in their deaths my grandparents were together again, and that perhaps my grandmother in choosing the time of her death had the solace of knowing she would be *close* to her beloved Sasha.

DER AELTESTE DER JUDEN
IN LITZMANNSTADT.

Abmeldung.

Familienname _____

Vornamen _____

Vornamen der Eltern _____

Stand _____ Geburtsort _____

Geburtsdatum _____ Religion _____

Beruf _____ Karten Nr. _____

Der Obengenannte verliess am _____

die Wohn. Nr. ___ an der _____

Nr. ___ Ursache _____

Neue Adresse _____

Anmerkungen : _____

Litzmannstadt-Getto, d. _____ 194_

Eigenhändige Unterschrift
des verantwortlichen Hausverwalters.

Eigenhändige Unterschrift des
Abgemeldeten oder Wohnungsinhabers.

Death certificate for mother Mera Rozin

Endnotes

1 In her letters my grandmother also uses Mania and Maria. Mera is the name on her birth certificate.

2 At the time of my grandmother's birth, Suwalki was part of the Russian Empire; from 1919 it was part of Poland until 1939. It is currently in Poland with a population of 69,210 and is close to the southwestern Lithuanian border.

3 To obtain a sense of the degradation of health in the ghetto, in 1938 before the war the death rate per thousand was 10.8; in 1942, it was 159.6 per thousand.

4 *Chronicle*, Introduction, xviii.

5 Ibid., xxix.

6 Trunk, *Lodz Ghetto: A History*, 15.

7 Ibid., 8.

8 Ibid., 15.

9 Ibid., 16.

10 Ibid., xxxi.

11 This letter is written in Polish. However, my grandmother uses German when referring to her request for money from a Berlin bank, assuming that this would help pass the censors. In fact, very early on, Germans forbade receipt of money from German banks. A local currency, "rumki," was established which could only be used within the ghetto. From the end of May 1940, outside funds were sent to the Litzmannstadt City Bank and were no longer available to the ghetto inhabitants who were forced to use only the internally approved currency.

12 The husband of my grandmother's sister-in law-Tania, both of whom were in Riga, then under the Soviet Union.

13 Janek was the only brother of my grandfather who survived the war. Many years before the war he converted in order to become a judge; Jews could be lawyers but not judges. I do not know what happened to his sisters who were in the Soviet Union and were not in communication with my parents before or after the war.

14 In between lines she writes in Polish, "don't send money for now," obviously fearing confiscation.

15 Trunk, 45.

16 Ibid.

17 She is referring to Artek, who fled to the Warsaw Ghetto with his wife and son.

18 I could not find out what is referred to here, but Henri could still be sending packages from Riga since the Germans did not invade the Soviet Union until August 1941.

19 The latter are not in the collection I have and likely were never sent by the German authorities, who intercepted mail frequently.

20 Horwitz, *Ghetto Stadt: Lodz and the Making of a Nazi City*, 97.

21 Trunk, 119.

22 Oscar Rosenfeld, *In the Beginning was the Ghetto*, Notebook A., 25.

23 Ibid., 25.

24 I do not know what money my grandmother is referring to since no one in the household was working and any money that people had was confiscated.

25 My parents saved several receipts of packages sent to both my grandmother and to my grandparents in the Warsaw Ghetto.

26 The Lodz Jewish cemetery was the largest Jewish cemetery in Europe, enclosed in the ghetto at the final drawing of the ghetto's boundaries, thus explaining my grandmother's visits to my grandfather's grave site.

27 Tania, Nunia, and Pepa are my grandfather's sisters, all of whom are Communists living in the Soviet Union.

28 Women who were not employed were put in charge of managing the apartments where they lived. This work was unpaid. It is clear from this postcard that my grandmother has assumed this responsibility and derives pride from her organizational skills.

29 Her brother was 10 years younger than she and still thinks of him "my good boy."

30 In fact, Uncle Love was a wealthy man, whose assets as noted in the affidavit for my parents in contemporary dollars would have amounted to a million dollars.

31 My grandmother is referring to an affidavit, which of course could not be provided under the circumstances. There was no "exit" from the ghetto other than deportation.

32 My mother's birthday was April 22. My grandmother must be sending these wishes in advance because of the uncertainty of the mail. She again sends birthday wishes on my mother's actual birthday.

33 Princova. I don't know this part of the family or how close she was to my father.

34 An interesting error. My father was two years younger than my mother, a fact that I believe my parents concealed from both of their parents. It was not considered appropriate then for the man to be younger than his wife.

35 Both Artek and my grandmother seem to think that even at this point in the war visas could be arranged for them.

36 Ghetto residents had to remain in their homes until the police arrived for the round-ups of children, the sick, and the aged.

37 The first deportation took place on December 20, 1941, when 20,000 were marked for deportation, including many who had recently arrived from Germany and Austria, as well as Gypsies from various areas. From January 16 to January 29, 1942, 10,103 were deported; between the end of February to the end of April, a total of 55,000 were deported in 66 transports. Trunk, *Lodz Ghetto: A History*, xlvii.

38 Horwitz, 209.

39 Ibid., 214.

40 Hell or a place of extreme torment. From the Bible, the valley of Hinnon, near Jerusalem where propitiatory sacrifices were made to Moloch (Kings 23:10).

Chapter 5

Voices of Despair—Letters From the Warsaw Ghetto, 1938–1941

The Warsaw Ghetto

After the Polish surrender, the Germans occupied Lodz, and those Jews who could, fled to Warsaw. Unlike Lodz, which was renamed Litzmannstadt and incorporated into the Third Reich, Warsaw was in the area of Poland under German jurisdiction but not considered part of Germany (the General Gouvernement). To those fleeing from the brutality of the German army in Lodz, Warsaw seemed like the "safer" city. In reality, Nazis were destructive and brutal everywhere.

Among those in my family who fled to Warsaw from Lodz were my father's parents, Aron and Roza Wolkowicz, along with my mother's Uncle Artek Rozin, his wife Hela, son Marchelek, and her cousin Adek (Arkadius Polakov), his wife Fela (Felicia), and daughter Anitka, who was born in 1938. The letters in this chapter are from these relatives. The chapter begins with a brief description of the Warsaw Ghetto conditions and how they differed from those in the Lodz Ghetto.

Family members quickly learned that Warsaw provided "no escape" from Nazi policies toward Jews either before the ghetto was established nor afterwards. Jews were starved, beaten, and ultimately confined within the ghetto during November 1940. At first, the Warsaw Ghetto circumstances were even harsher than those in the Lodz Ghetto. There were fewer opportunities for employment, and starvation was even more pressing. The Germans officially approved 184 calories per person a day in food supplied by them. For the starving population to be fed, smuggling became the only answer.

Before the war, Jews comprised 30 percent of Warsaw's population of 400,000. They and those who fled from Lodz and other cities to Warsaw were crammed into 2.4 percent of Warsaw's housing in an area of 1.3 square miles. As in the Lodz Ghetto, the fundamental cause of the diseases that took the lives of so many were the overcrowded living conditions and starvation. In the month of January 1938 before the ghetto was established, the mortality figure among Jews in Warsaw was 454; by January 1942 it was 5,123.

Unlike the Lodz Ghetto, which was hermetically sealed with police inside and outside shooting anyone who attempted to escape, and where smuggling was impossible and punished by a death sentence, smuggling in the Warsaw Ghetto—although dangerous—occurred all the time, often carried out by small children who could squeeze through small openings in the walls.

Again, unlike the Lodz Ghetto whose archives formed the basis of the *Lodz Chronicle* documented and written by Jewish administrators, the Warsaw Ghetto had a secret, underground documentation project led by the historian, political activist, and social worker Emanuel Ringelblum under the code name of Oneg Shabat [meaning Joyous Sabbath]. Its goal was to document daily events and preserve documents for the purpose of sending reports to the Polish Underground and Polish Government in Exile, and ultimately to tell the world about the horrors that were occurring.

To do this, Ringelblum secretly enlisted Jewish writers, scientists, and ordinary people to gather documents, diaries, decrees, and other documents. He was also one of the most active members of Alynhilf, a Jewish self-help organization consisting of social workers, intellectuals, and journalists, whose goal was to maintain a "sense of communal responsibility and social solidarity" within the ghetto.[1]

When the Warsaw Ghetto uprising occurred in April and May 1943, the archives included more than 25,000 pages of documentation constituting a wide variety of reports about every aspect of ghetto life as well as deportations, including those from other towns. These documents were hidden in boxes and three large milk canisters that were buried to preserve them for future generations. Most of the boxes and two of the milk cans were recovered after the war and provide a remarkable history of the Warsaw Ghetto that unlike the Chronicle of the Lodz Ghetto which was written with the knowledge that Germans might read it was written from the point of view of the victims.

Ringelblum and his family went into hiding before the ghetto uprising, but his hiding place was revealed by informants, and on March 7, 1944, they were all arrested and shot. The Jewish Historical Institute in Warsaw is named in his honor and has the major collection of documents concerning the Warsaw Ghetto.

The major deportations from the Warsaw Ghetto to extermination camps began in July 1942. Like the deportations from Lodz, exceptions to deportations included members of the Jewish Council, which was the administrative body of the ghetto, and the Jewish police, doctors, nurses, and close family members of any of these professions. On July 22, 1942, the Aktion began. When it was completed, 265,000 of the inhabitants had been sent to Treblinka's gas chambers to die; 11,580 were sent to labor camps. The deportations lasted until September 12, 1942.

The leader of the Warsaw Ghetto, Adam Czerniakov, whose position as head of the ghetto, like that of Rumkovski in the Lodz Ghetto, required him to carry out Nazi orders. Rather than send the inhabitants to what he knew to be certain deaths, he committed suicide on July 23, 1942. He left two notes: one to his wife and one to the governing body of the ghetto, the Jewish Council. He wrote that that the German administrators had informed him that among the 4,000 [or possibly 9,000; his message was not clear] whom he was asked to deport were children. He asked the Council not to view his suicide as an act of cowardice. He could not hand over children to their deaths. In his note, he wrote, "I am powerless, my heart trembles in sorrow and compassion. I can no longer bear all this. My act will show everyone the right thing to do."[2] He did not sign the expulsion order.

After September 1942, only 35,000 were allowed to remain, mostly young and single people. However, another 20,000 remained in hiding. When the next deportation was announced in January 1943, the two underground defense groups that had begun to organize in July 1942, the ZOB (Jewish Combat Organization representing leftwing parties) and ZZW (Jewish Military Union) representing rightwing Zionists united to defend themselves in an uprising against another deportation. After seizing 5,000 to 6,500 inhabitants the Germans suspended further deportations.

In the event that the Germans would organize a final deportation, the remaining Jews began to construct subterranean bunkers and shelters in preparation for another uprising. The operation to liquidate the ghetto began on April 19, 1943, during Passover. Virtually the entire population had gone into hiding. Although ultimately the Germans overcame the resistance, it continued for almost a month before the ghetto was liquidated and the remaining Jews sent to Treblinka.

I don't know when or how my relatives died or if they were transported to Treblinka. Unlike Auschwitz from which the Germans fled near the end of the war and whose structures remained, Treblinka, located 50 miles from Warsaw in a rural area which is still sparsely populated, was blown up and destroyed in 1943 to hide all traces of what went on there. There are no records of those who entered and were killed in the gas chambers. Like Auschwitz-Birkenau, Treblinka II was solely an extermination camp.[3] The victims went from the train station to rooms where their hair was shorn and clothes removed, and they were taken directly to the gas chambers.

Letters from the Warsaw Ghetto

The letters are from three time periods: 1) immediately before the Germans invaded Poland in 1939; 2) after the Germans occupied Warsaw but before the ghetto was sealed; and 3) from November 16, 1940, when the Warsaw Ghetto was officially sealed, until October 8, 1941, the date of the last letter that my parents received from their relatives in the Warsaw Ghetto.

The letters that my parents received from the Warsaw Ghetto all asked for food, clothing, and affidavits to help them flee from their dire circumstances. No one in the family survived. If they lived until the transports of July to September 1942, they would have died in the gas chambers in Treblinka. I do not know which fate they met.

The letters came from my father's parents, Roza and Aron Wolkowicz; my mother's uncle Artek; and my mother's cousin Adek, whom she described to me as her childhood playmate and partner in mischief. I begin with the letters from Adek.

Adek's first letter to my parents was from Lodz, written before the war in December 1938. He admits that he is full of envy of their good fortune to be "taken by Uncle Love" to the U.S. Much of the letter is filled with the good news that his wife Fela has given birth to a baby girl, Anitka. The rest of the letter is directed to my mother whom he suggested could assist him in his export business in scarves and kerchiefs—products that Poland was known for and that were highly desired in the States. He asks that she become his agent and research what styles could be exported to the States.

Apparently my parents had written that their situation with Uncle Love was not what they had hoped. Adek responds to their complaints that compared with what was happening in Poland they should be glad to be there.

December 8, 1938

What Mikhal writes is perhaps sad; he is certainly disappointed, because it was supposed to be one way and it turned out quite different. But it is good! I don't want to moralize, I only state the fact. In my opinion, you are lucky. This is the way it is. Personally, I believe that everything else is just some minor issues. They aren't worth worrying about — you are free in a free country. I know your indomitable energy and I can imagine you in the future. I believe that your temporary disappointment will be abundantly made up for in the future.

At the end of his long letter, mainly about soliciting my mother's help in developing an export business in scarves and kerchiefs, he alludes to what is happening in Europe.

As far as everyday things are concerned, I can only tell you that I can't stand to take a newspaper in my hands. We are beaten over here, killed over there, confiscated here, etc. You surely know all about that. Business is going somehow, but you could feel what I mentioned above.

The next letter is from Warsaw where he has fled with his wife Fela. The ghetto has not yet been established.

August 8, 1940

My dear ones, Unfortunately, I am not able to get in touch with you in any way, This is all the sadder, as I wanted to let Mania [my mother's mother, named by one of her many nicknames, and his aunt] *know that you are alive. That would keep her spirits up in these hard times. Mania and my parents are still in Lodz, but we get regular news from them. She is healthy and she is doing well. She would be happy if she could be together with you. You should try to arrange that. I am surprised that you don't make an effort to write, especially since letters, packages and even money get through. You can also write through the Red Cross and through the Joint Distribution Committee.*

Postcard from my mother's cousin Adek Polakov from the Warsaw Ghetto

Please write every week so that we can stay in touch. This would be highly desirable. Please write to Mania using my Warsaw address; do it for sure. We are healthy, thank God and our Anitka is all grown up.

Photo of Anitka Polakov slipped in with the letter

He also asks that they send packages because registered packages are getting through. And he talks of other family members, but it is clear that he doesn't want to name their actual locations since all of the letters were censored, as marked on the envelopes.

We are waiting for your news. Please write every week so we have regular contact. Is there any possibility to see you?!! Please forward our greetings to Doctor [he is referring to Uncle Love].

I send my kisses,
Adek

This letter is the last one my parents will ever receive from Adek. I was told that he and his wife, who was not Jewish, tried to escape the ghetto, and were shot on the spot. My parents tried to locate Anitka after the war but could not get information about her. When I visited Poland in 2012, I went to the Center for Jewish History in Warsaw and inquired about how I might go about finding Anitka if she was still alive. The woman in charge discouraged me. First, of course, I did not know Anitka's last name. If her parents had perished and she was given to others to care for, most likely her name would have been changed.

More importantly she asked, "And if you find her, what would you do? She may not want to have anything to do with you or she may desperately need your help." I was taken aback by her reply. I realized that I had constructed a fantasy image of recovering a long lost relative, not much older than I am. Because of my fantasy, I had not considered these questions. Ultimately, I chose not to try and find Anitka. However I found out something very important and interesting about her parents when I went to Lodz.

With my translator, Ela Gugula, I went to Lodz's Office of Civil Records, taking a long ride on a tram to a deserted part of town. When I submitted my request for information regarding the marriage date of Adek (Arkadius Polakov) and his wife, Felicia (Fela), the clerk told me that she had this information but that I was not a close enough relative to receive it. I asked Ela to let her know that I had come all the way from the United States to obtain this information. The women left the desk and returned with a slip of paper, which she pushed under the window separating us. On it was Anitka's mother's maiden name, Felicja Sendowicz Zerykier, and also Adek's and Fela's marriage date, December 21, 1938.

This was not their actual marriage date. Since I knew when Anitka was born, and this date was after her birth, I realized that to protect her, Adek and Fela had married officially in the Catholic Church at the end of 1938. Jewish weddings were not recorded in the official records; only Catholic marriages were documented. They had married to protect their child whom they registered as a baptized Catholic. Anitka may have survived and been raised by a Catholic family.

Artek, my mother's uncle, his wife Ester, and child Marchelek, were also in Warsaw. Artek served in the army when Poland was invaded, was briefly imprisoned and was able to return to his family and flee with them to Warsaw. His first postcard--letters could rarely pass the German censors—is dated September 6, 1940—which is before the sealing of the ghetto in November of that year. In it he lets my parents know the extreme conditions in which he and his family are living:

September 6, 1940

My Dears,

I have already written several letters to you, but I haven't received any answer from you. Unfortunately, I haven't been able to correspond with Mania [my grandmother in Lodz] *yet and I don't know how things are with her. I am asking you very much to take us to you. I mean me, my wife Ester, and my son Marcel. Here we are without any means to survive. We in a very harsh situation. Marchelek lost weight, he doesn't go to school, my brother-in-law Herman died.*

I am specifically asking for an immediate answer and speedy help. How is Aunt and Uncle? What are you up to? Mikhal's parents are in Warsaw and they complain about the lack of information from you.

Kisses,
Artek

Although the ghetto was not yet enclosed, the street address is located where the future ghetto will be, which was in Warsaw's Jewish district.

The next letter is written from another address after the establishment of the ghetto.

December 8, 1940

My Dears,

I am still without news from you. I am impatiently awaiting your letters. How is Uncle's health? What is going on with you? I received a food package from Riga. Was it from you? I am without work. Help is necessary. Unfortunately, I cannot get in touch with Mania since my return from captivity. I only know that she is with Dora in Lodz.

> *Can't you take us to you? I am begging you for letters and material help. Don't forget about us. Mikhal's parents are in Warsaw. I see them often.*

> *I kiss Aunt, Uncle and You very tenderly,*
> *Artek, Hela and Marchelek*

I want to believe that my parents responded to both of these letters, and that their letters were confiscated, as the Germans routinely did. I also want to believe that the package came from them.

The final letter comes five months later in April 1941. Again desperate, Artek acknowledges the receipt of a package which came via Bulgaria, a neutral country in the war through which letters and packages could get through.

> *April 27, 1941*

> *My Dears!*

> *Today we received a package from you from Bulgaria. Because of the changing of our address the package took a long time to get to us, but everything came intact and was very useful. We are asking you so much for further help, perhaps through Portugal* [another neutral country]. *It is specifically important for Marchelek. I am making a minimal amount of money and it's very hard for us to make ends meet. I get letters from Mania. She also had troubles surviving. Your help is also necessary for her. Are there any possibilities of immigration to you? Don't forget us.*

> *How is the health of dear Uncle and Aunt? I am also writing a postcard at their address. Our family in Russia is doing well, but they seldom write to us, and don't send packages at all.*

> *I kiss you tenderly,*
> *Artek*

This is the last letter that my parents received from Artek. I do not know whether or how hard my parents tried to help. My mother was very close to her uncle, but she never told me what happened to him, Ester, and Marchelek. I never heard her mention their names. The silence may speak to her sadness and also to her not having done enough.

My paternal grandparents, Aron and Roza Wolkowicz, also wrote from the Warsaw Ghetto and were in touch with other members of the family in Lodz. Neither of them wrote in Polish or German with any fluency. There are four postcards from them—all written in 1941 in Polish, shortly after the ghetto was sealed. They are all sent from the same address, Walicov 7, apt. 6. Since my grandparents acknowledge a package sent via Bulgaria, clearly my parents had written to them before these postcards arrived.

January 22, 1941 My dearest ones!

We wrote you three registered letters via air mail, and we got no response. On the 20ᵗʰ of January, we received a package from Sophia, Bulgaria [capital of Bulgaria, the neutral country through which they communicated] *for which we thank you. We wrote back right away to let you know that we got it. We ask you to keep sending us the packages because they keep us alive. It weighed four and a half kilograms and I enumerated all that was in it.*

We ask you for tea and cocoa and please don't wait with it because we need it urgently. Besides that, how are you and how is your health? How is your new practice doing? We ask you to answer promptly.

We send our greetings and hundreds of kisses from your parents,

Roza Wolkowicz

We ask you to keep sending us the packages because they keep us alive.

Did my parents understand? Could anyone have understood? Certainly packages were intercepted and destroyed by the Germans. We know this. Did my parents or grandparents understand this? The next postcard arrives two month later.

March 11, 1941 My Dearest Ones!

We received your letter dated January 17 and received your package from Sophia [Bulgaria] *on the 20ᵗʰ of January. We wrote right back via Sophia and we also wrote what was in the package. If it is not too hard please keep sending us packages via Stockholm.*

We are very hurt that Uncle Love hardly helped you with anything. You had recently many expenses. Please write what you heard from Uncle Jozef [I don't know the uncle that my grandmother refers to]. *We send our greetings and kiss you warmly. Please write back promptly.*

My kisses, your Mother [in Polish the word for mother would be capitalized, "Matka"],

Roza Wolkowicz.

Clearly my grandparents were starving, but like my maternal grandmother, they also try to imagine their children's lives and sympathize with their good news. The story of Uncle Love not helping my parents is a consistent theme in their letters to their parents. Had my parents understood their condition of near starvation, they probably would not have sent such news about Uncle Love. But they could not have known or understood. My reading of the letters is so painful because I do know that my grandparents were starving and had no money. By this time all valuables and money had been confiscated, as it was in the Lodz Ghetto, and it is unlikely that either of them was employed.

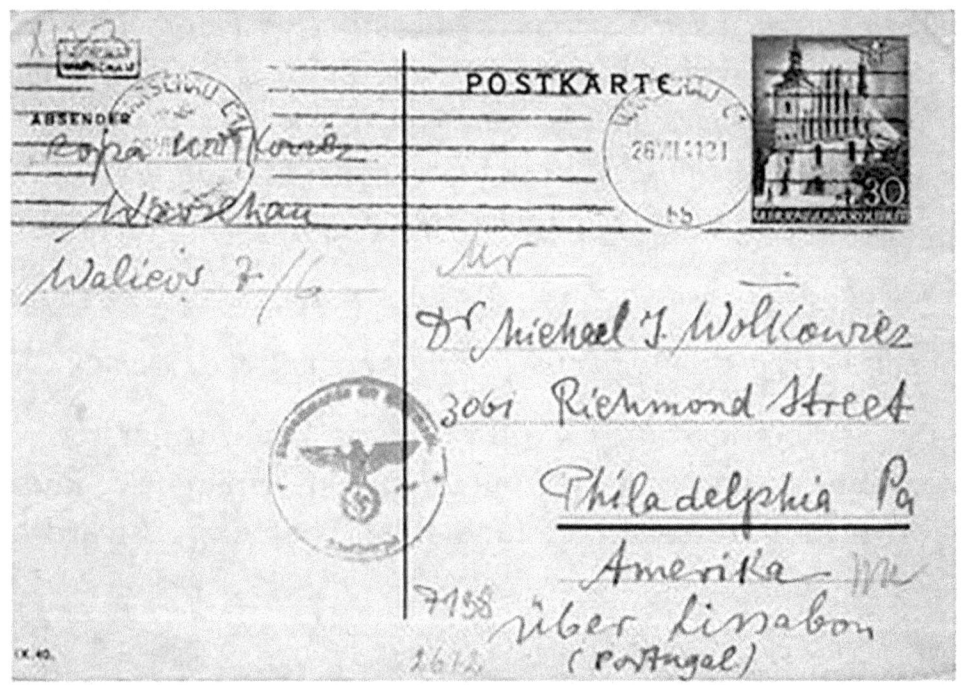

Postcard from Father's parents telling them where to send packages via Portugal

The next postcard to my parents, dated July 24, 1941, is focused on how to send packages through Portugal with two possible addresses that were forwarding food to the Warsaw Ghetto.

> *We ask you to fill the packages with nothing else but . 5 kilograms of vanilla sticks, cocoa, tea and cofiee beans.*

The last postcard my parents ever received from my father's parents in Warsaw was dated October 8, 1941. This one is written by my grandfather, and the warm tone is immediately noticeable and different from my grandmother Roza's.

October 8, 1941

My Dearest Ones!

After five months we have finally received your air mail postcard. It gave us such pleasure to read it and all the news brings us joy, especially from Hala. Also we are so happy that you will own a house and have a car. As far as the packages are concerned, we could very much use them and send them to us as quickly as possible. When it comes to us we are still alive.

I kiss you and hug you tightly. Your Father Aron.

Best regards to your uncle and his family. We wish you all the best for your wedding anniversary. Regards and kisses from your mother,

Rozalja

The good news mentioned in this letter is that my mother was pregnant with me. The tone of this letter is moving. My grandfather clearly tries to celebrate their good news—a baby on the way, a house, and a car. But he must also state the reality of their own lives: *When it comes to us, we are still alive.* He might have written the truth, "barely alive."

I am moved that my paternal grandparents knew that their children were thriving and expecting a child. The last postcard from my grandfather Aron reflected their satisfaction in knowing that their children would be fine-- they have created a new life for themselves, and they are expecting a child. In the desperate times of October 1941 in the Warsaw Ghetto they had news that gave them joy.

The diary entry by Czerniakov on the day my grandfather wrote his final letter to my parents notes the following about food shortages:

> *Bischof* [the German official in charge of the Warsaw Ghetto to whom Czerniakow, the head of the Judenrat, reported] *telephoned about the parcels requisitioned at the post ofiice. During September 15,000 parcels, with an estimated value of several million zloty were requisitioned. They requisition parcels over 6 pounds if they contain leather, flour, fats; under 4 pounds if there are several for one addressee.*[4]

I include this information because my grandparents were apparently aware that packages containing certain foods were requisitioned by the Germans. Therefore, they asked their children for things that would not be requisitioned such as tea and coffee.

If my grandparents had survived until 1942 they would have been transported to Treblinka to be sent immediately from the train to the gas chambers. It is located 50 miles from Warsaw in a rural part of Poland that consists mainly of small farms. Treblinka itself has been "memorialized" in a moving way. Accompanied by my husband and Ela, I visited Treblinka during my trip to Poland in 2012.

These are the notes I wrote about my visit to Treblinka II:[5]

> We walked down a winding dirt road through a forest that opens to a grassy field. In the center is a rough-hewn, massive stone structure to memorialize the victims who met their deaths here. Scattered throughout the field are 17,000 large, jagged stones which are positioned randomly to remind visitors of the horror that this bucolic site was used for--an efficient killing machine that destroyed approximately 800,000 Jews between 1941 and 1943.[6] I placed a stone at the base of the central stone monument to the dead inscribed with the words "Never Again." Many visitors place stones in memory and respect of those who died here.

The Nazis designed the entrance to the camp to look like an ordinary railroad station in order to deceive the terrified and bewildered men, women, and children pouring out from the cattle cars, and thus prevent panic and rioting. At the station the men and women were immediately separated and directed to the "changing rooms" where they were shaved and their clothes taken away. From there they were told they were going to take showers for delousing, and they passed nude through a "garlanded" gate — designed to prevent panic. The rest *is* known.

I walked in Treblinka for a long time, leaving my husband and Ela to their own devices. I needed to be alone with the remains of those buried there. I knew my paternal grandparents only from a photograph and bits and pieces of my father's memories that he shared with me. I cried in Treblinka for the first time in Poland as I thought about the end for two older people, so incredibly proud of their son in America, facing this brutal death with no way to reach him. No opportunity to say good-bye or to have a final word with him.

I felt so sad for my father who lived with the terrible knowledge of their end. Since my father never visited Treblinka it was only recently established as a memorial to the Jews who died here I doubt that he ever knew the exact "science of extermination" that was practiced. I was glad that my parents were saved from such knowledge.

Treblinka-Lodz Monument

Endnotes

1 Sloan, ed. *Notes from the Warsaw Ghetto: The Journal of Emanuel Ringelblum*, ix-xxvii.

2 Hilberg, *The Warsaw Diary of Adam Czerniakow: Prelude to Doom*, 23.

3 It is estimated that 800,000 Jews and 2000 Romani were killed at Treblinka II, a number only surpassed by Auschwitz. There was also a forced labor camp, Treblinka I.

4 Hilberg, 286.

5 The German abandoned Treblinka II in 1943 because they were concerned its purpose would become known. The bones of the gassed victims were buried in the ground. The estimate of the numbers involved was based on the skeletons that were unearthed.

6 The exact numbers are not known because the Germans destroyed all traces before abandoning it; the numbers are estimated from survivors' reports and the remains that were found buried. It is estimated that of the 800,000, 67 survived.

Chapter 6

Letters From a Friend — Bolek Bejslechem, 1939–1946

Bolek Bejslechem[1]

When I first met Bolek I was fifteen. I was traveling with my parents on my first trip to Europe in 1955. This was also their first time back to Europe since they had left in April 1938. My father introduced him as his best friend and schoolmate from Lodz and later from medical school in Paris. By this time he was a country doctor in a village outside Paris.

Bolek Bejslechem and his wife Toshka, Paris, 12/31/45

As soon as I met Bolek, I liked him. He didn't speak English, and my French was not fluent, but I sensed his gentleness and his and my father's affection for one another. When they were together there was a mutual understanding and warmth that I rarely saw with most of my parents' American friends. My father was always polite, charming, and formal. He was familiarly called the "prince" in the hospital, perhaps with a touch of irony. In his later years, he developed a nervous facial tic resulting, I believe, from his vigilant self-control. With Bolek, and a few other friends from his childhood, he was different.

Bolek' home and office were in an old stone house surrounded by a garden. Three small rooms — a waiting room and two examining rooms — were devoted to his practice. The contrast with my parents' life in the U.S. was startling. By 1955, my father, an ophthalmologist, worked in three hospitals and had two offices in Philadelphia.

At the time, I thought Bolek's life in the country was preferable, the one that I would have liked. I knew nothing of his life during the war or of his narrow escape from becoming a German prisoner. He and his wife Toshka had a child of five, Jean Noel, adopted from a Catholic Orphanage. He was a beautiful boy, gentle like his father.

After this visit, I had no contact with Bolek, but my parents stayed in touch, and eventually he and Toshka visited my parents in the U.S. Years later, my parents called to tell me that Bolek and Toshka had committed suicide together. He had congestive heart failure, and his suffering had become unbearable.

When I read Bolek's letters, I discovered a caring man, with a capacity for deep friendship, willing to help my father when his own life and livelihood were endangered. He was also a gifted letter writer, able to convey his emotions and provide vivid descriptions of his life even in desperate and dangerous times.

The first letter is dated October 13, 1939. By this time, my parents had been living in the States for over a year. The last letter is dated April 2, 1946. This chapter is divided into two parts--Part I: Love and War, October 1939 December 1940, and Part II: Post-War Hopes, December, 1945 April 1946.

Part I: Love and War–October 1939– December 1940

The first two letters are about Rose, a close friend of my parents, whom they sent "to meet Bolek" in Paris on a kind of transcontinental "blind date." Bolek writes that they were smitten with each other right away, and that Rosa — as he calls her — and he had decided to marry. The outbreak of the war in Poland on

September 1, 1939 and the subsequent declaration of war by France and England against Germany thwarted their plans. For her safety, Bolek insisted that Rose return to the U.S., which she did reluctantly on October 15, 1939. They planned to reunite after the war but never did.

Rose was a close family friend, whom I knew and loved. She was an independent, single woman who, with her brother, ran their family's furniture store. She was close to my parents, loved to joke often in Yiddish and always dressed stylishly. She was short and petite, with thick reddish blond hair. When my parents traveled to medical conferencesusually an opportunity for a brief vacation Rose would stay with me. I wanted to be like Rose.

The discovery that my parents arranged for Bolek's and Rose's meeting in Paris, and that they were forced apart because of the war after a passionate love affair, stunned me. I speculated that this may have contributed to Rose's decision not to marry, since perhaps Bolek was the "love of her life." Her encounter with the threat of war and awareness of the fate of Jews in Europe contributed to her change of name from "Kessler," which Bolek used in his letters, to the non-Jewish-sounding name "Harrison," which is the name I knew.

Later in October, Bolek again writes of his feelings for Rose and his sadness following her return to the States. He is without work and Paris *is* preparing for war. The letter is long and tragic, worth quoting in its entirety because it reveals so much about Bolek and about the grim preparations for war in Paris. The final letter in Part I is from July 1940 when as a soldier in the Polish Army in France, he fled before an oncoming German attack on his battalion to Agen, a small town in the South, where he stayed briefly before returning to Paris.

Following this there is no further correspondence between my parents and Bolek until 1945, one year after the war ended in France. This exchange is very unlike any in the earlier years. Tragedy and loss are not the focus of the first two letters but do emerge sharply in the final letter, written in 1946. Almost everyone in my parents' families and in Bolek's had died. By 1946, he wants to leave France, a country in which he survived but which he does not see as welcoming and where he feels that he cannot thrive. The letters end with no resolution in sight for Bolek. He clearly recognizes the barriers to emigration at this point not the least of them being the number of years that would be required to be licensed as a physician in the U.S.

Paris, October 13, 1939

My dear Mikhal and Hala,

This is the third letter I am writing to you since the outbreak of the war, but I suspect that you didn't get any from me so far. The first letter was quite short and sad. I was writing under the influence of the sad incidents that took place recently. I sent it on September 20th by regular mail. I sent the second letter to Miss Kessler; it is very detailed and will give you the overview of the entire situation. She is leaving Paris on October 15th, so you will not receive it before the end of the month. I can't write everything that I wrote in previous letters, but I will try and satisfy your curiosity and give you a short summary of what I have already written.

You probably can guess how things with Rosa and me stand. We took a liking to each other spontaneously and without anybody's suggestion. Indeed, it was a wonderful occurrence in our lives and we felt like we were made for each other.[2] War put an end to our idyll. We gave each other our word that the war interrupted only temporarily what had to happen. And she left very unwillingly and mainly because of my pressure. So that the matter is unchanged, and as soon as circumstances allow, she will come back to Europe.

When it comes to my life, I am not doing well, as is the case with everyone. I no longer work in the hospital, but still have evening consultations, which bring me 200 francs a month.[3] It is hard to get work, although it seems paradoxical. They don't want to take drafted men any where, and if you want to get employment, you have to show documents that you are free from army duty. When it comes to the army matter, you probably know that all Polish citizens similarly to Frenchmen, are under obligation to perform army service. I am to appear at the army headquarters on the 20th of October, and later I will probably be sent to ofiicer's school. But this matter will probably take a few weeks.

Please calm Rosa because she probably thinks I am in the trenches already. I have news from Michnik.[4] Obviously he is at the front, but not in the place where they are fighting. So far he has not heard a single shot. I spoke to his wife. She is very depressed and down about all of this.

I am doing nothing. I walk the streets and all my actions consist of waiting and waiting. Poverty reigns among our friends, and everybody is doing what they can while they await the draft. I am in deep debt. I walk around the streets, and discuss matters on street corners. I am followed by the memory of Rosa, the memory of my sad war romance.

I went to the Red Cross to find out about my parents.[5] Nothing! Mikhal and Hala, please write to me. I so much long for news from you.

Bolek

At the end of October 1939 Bolek again writes of his feelings about the loss of Rose, and his despair. This letter has only the month and year. Since I don't have an envelope for it, I assume it followed the letter of October 13.

My Dears,

The last courier from Europe Miss Kessler. How it all strongly twists and turns. And so pass the years of wandering and toil, and so crumble to ashes and dust the soaring edifices of dreams... you have surely received my last letter; sad, so very sad. Today I will try to introduce a happier note into my thoughts. Recollections of Rosa flutter in my heart. How strange it all is. I didn't expect to go through so many wonderful moments with her.

Everything between us was born so spontaneously and suddenly. And we had dreams and the land of happiness was just about to open before me. We were barely two weeks together. Two weeks. Years pass sometimes without brilliance, glum and monotonous. And for two weeks – so much happiness. Today my most ardent desire is for the nightmare to perish and for the destructive elements to calm. Rosa will come back once again and we will experience this wonderful idyll for the second time.

She was leaving this old Europe with a broken heart but she knew that she would return and it would be our most beautiful story of all. And indeed, everything unfolds as in a story. Rusty wheels of history spin again and the course of events leaps forward with a blazing speed. Caught in the mad whirlpool, I feel insignificant, a speck of dust, without direction and without helm I am thrust onto raging waves. What of it that I can feel and think, and love? Soon I will be like the other millions who put on their soldiers' uniforms and join the ranks. I will keep on writing to you. You are everything that is dearest and closest to me now. If anything should happen to me you will be notified, and I submitted your address. But I am not joining the ranks with that thought in mind. I want to live more than ever, and I believe that we will see each other again. These hard days will pass and the horizon will brighten again.

Michał, Hala, not a day goes past without my talking and thinking about you. With affection, I recall the moments we spent together in Paris. How strangely has fate directed our routes! It is a great relief for me, however, to think that I have friends who think and care about me in Philadelphia. I am fully aware how lonely I am in Paris. Everyone is gradually dispersing. Some leave Paris in panic, others get drafted into the ranks. I assume I will be drafted into the ranks of the Polish Army in France this month. Polish citizens are mobilized and are subject to a general duty of military service.

Oh how this Paris differs from the one you know. When the night falls, there are no more light-flooded boulevards, there are no more colorful advertisements; everything is engulfed by a thick darkness. Only every so often tiny blue lights are twinkling, and nights are fearfully dark, torn by grim cries of sirens. But the days are still sunny. Empty streets are watching through their facades of closed businesses. Windows with their pasted paper paint a strange picture. Every few steps you are ambushed by a bomb shelter. In the Luxembourg Gardens they keep digging trenches and placing anti-aircraft cannons. And everywhere, but everywhere there rise the carts with sand. There are plenty of them, on the streets, at homes. They surround Notre Dame and all historical art places in Paris in a thick mass. People stroll around with gas masks on their shoulders, policemen in helmets stop young men in the streets to verify their military papers.

I don't work, I was released from the hospital.

Two times a week I have evening consultations. Others don't have that and they live in terrible poverty. So far it is not possible to find any work. They don't accept mobilized men anywhere. Everyone is then waiting for their new military life, and I belong in this group as well.

I roam the streets and think about my Rosa and about our sad war-time romance. I think about you and all the trouble you went through for me. I think about my parents and my sister from whom I have no news. I think that I roam the road that leads me "vers mon destin inconnu" [toward my unknown destination].

Bolek

P. S. Mikhal and Hala, I wanted to ask you to write to me as often as you can. Best thing via air-mail, as it takes only eight days to receive a letter. One needs to count on five to six weeks for the mail sent by ship nowadays. I will write to you often, whenever my fate should take me. Please write

*about everything you do. Do you see Rosa often? Do you talk about me?
How strangely my life falls. But believe me, in the most tragic situations I
will not extinguish this spark of instinct that propels me towards life and
optimism. And that is why I believe that the storm will pass above my head,
and that Rosa won't forget and keep her word, and that all of us, finally and
after so many obstacles, will meet again. Perhaps I lack a sense of realism
in thinking this way but I think that my considerations are the result of
a natural self- preservation instinct. I see that in my post scriptum I am
starting to veer towards a philosophical tract. Therefore I will finish and
I will impatiently wait for the news from you. I am curious how you will
judge it all, and what you think about all of this!*

Bolek

Paris, November 16, 1939

My dear Mikhal and Hala,

*Finally after many long weeks, I received some news from you. I don't
want "to play arithmetic" but in any case this is my fourth letter since the
outbreak of the war. I received your letter yesterday, and you can't accuse
me of being lazy when it comes to responding. Mikhal, you can rest assured,
all your things will be taken care of.[6] I will see to that. Don't doubt it for a
second. I can probably do it myself for you, because I will stay in Paris for
the next few months for sure.*

*The Polish army doesn't need doctors yet, and they will let me know
when they will need me. I am not pleased with this state of things and you
can guess why. I don't work, I eat my dinners in a "soup kitchen" for one
franc. To tell the truth, I am not the only one, and at the table I meet the
entire elite of "Parisian doctors." I blame myself that I didn't think about
America before and lately I am very depressed by it all. The hospital service
is closed for now. In other words, I don't know if my life will amount to
anything.*

*Ignace[7] stays in Paris and is being reformed and his life as usual is spent
on cooking and women. But these are his usual aspirations and they satisfy
him. Jerzy left a few days ago to join the army, the Foreign Legion. Don't be
afraid. This is the name of the army formation where they accept foreigners.
He doesn't know if he will be a doctor. Mojzesz[8] is somewhere "a l'Est."*

[in the East]. And I wander around lonely and as usual knocking on the Parisian cobblestones with my soles full of holes. And the years pass by....

I was hoping that the fall of 1939 would be a turning point in my life, but in reality I am in the same situation of waiting. I think about

Rosa. I think that your point of view is correct and I don't entertain too many illusions. But we really became very close, in every respect, and we simply didn't realize that the situation would turn this way. And it boosts my male ego that this reserved American woman became so enamored that she lost her balance and ability to reason. She wanted to stay, to marry me, but it doesn't matter, it's an old song. The future will show and for now I must treat the matter with utmost reserve.

But there is another meaning in this story. If it weren't for Rosa, I would be in Poland now, and who knows what would be going on with me. For now, Rosa played her part in my life. And nobody can predict what will happen later, where we are going, what is our goal, and what land we will find ourselves on because of this turmoil.

My heart is breaking when I think about my poor parents and my little sister. You, who know my life from close up, and now from far away, please write me frequently. I sense that you think about me a lot and I consider you the people who are closest to me.

I would like to send this letter via air mail, but it is really impossible. I feel hurt by Hala's silence in this situation, she could write a few words. I suppose that Rosa conveyed to you in detail the situation here. I sent a bottle of perfume with her for Hala. I hope she liked it. Mikhal, Hala I would so much like to see you, be with you, that sometimes I dream about it at night. America, the land of my dreams! But who knows if we will see each other.

Hugs,
Bolek

My mother's failure to write a few words of thanks to Bolek and acknowledge his thoughtfulness in sending her a gift is troubling to me, but not surprising. Throughout my mother's life, her focus was on my father, and he was always the one who was interested in sustaining friendships, especially those from his youth.

The next letter holds better news. Bolek is working again; he yearns for Rose but knows this is not possible, not yet. Its tone is much more optimistic, and Bolek encourages my father, who has to pass his exam following his internship in the U.S.

The letter is also optimistic about the end of the war, and clearly Bolek who has now heard from his parents in Lodz through censored letters, has no clear idea about the horrific conditions in Lodz following the German takeover of the city in October 1939. By February 1940 it was "hell" for Jews who were fleeing from one temporary housing to another, under a strict curfew, ordered to wear the Jewish "yellow star" at all times, and derided and abused by Nazi soldiers on the streets. Clearly, he nor my parents could have known this, and in Paris Bolek's life has stabilized.

Paris, February 3, 1940

My dears,

If you only knew how much pleasure I get from your letters, you would surely write to me more often. It's going on three years since our parting, but I don't feel this three-year long gap; for me you stayed the same. When I sometimes go back in my mind to our old Parisian times, when I speak about years which passed, never to return, I always add with melancholy, "A long time ago when Mikhal and Hala were here, it was difierent...." It's completely difierent today and our fates have pushed onto to very difierent roads.

For now my life somehow became more stable. I work at the ophthalmology department, and twice a week I have a consultation in internal diseases. Luckily, I have some work. I make ends meet, which is quite difiicult in present conditions. But I am certain that this month I will be drafted. Many of my friends already got their cards and I will surely not avoid this fate. I am sure that Rosa told you that I received a letter from my cousins in Riga;[9] they received a letter from my parents who are in Lodz. All this news made me very happy. Besides you can imagine how life goes by. We are waiting for big events, for the end of the war... I correspond with Rosa and we are also waiting for the end of the war. But I have a feeling that I will have to wait for a long time. But really, it's hard to predict anything at present. Sometimes I imagine that you are sitting in front of the fire place in Philadelphia in the evening. Rosa is with you, and you are talking about me, about the storm that broke over Europe. How I would like to be among you, my old, and faithful friends, in the warm atmosphere of people who are close to me.

But for now I am far away from you and sometimes wonder if in the fast American life, you still remember your old friend Bolek. Write to me.

Perhaps soon fate will throw me into this turmoil and it will be hard to stay in touch.

I already wrote you about my life. I am rather busy all day long. In the evenings I often go to Jacques and Lucy my new French friends. They often invite me for dinner and this is how life goes on, without thunders, among small problems and small pleasures.

Write me what's going on with you. I am sure that Mikhal will pass his exams. I believe it without a doubt. What do you do in your free moments? Do you have a lot of friends? Does Rosa visit you often? What plans do you have for the future? I am sure that you will get a letter from your parents, gradually everyone starts getting news.

I am finishing and asking you not to delay with your answer.

Hugs,

Bolek

Kind greetings for Uncle and Aunt Love. Thank you for the money, but I really don't need it right now. I manage somehow. I am waiting for news from you.

The next letter from March 13, 1940, concerns my father's request for his medical records. He has asked Bolek to track them down for him in Paris. Without them he cannot practice in the U.S.

Bolek writes:

The chair of his department as an exception decided to issue the document you need. I will get the certificate from the secretary in a few days. Formalities concerning legalization will take me ten days because ministries were moved to the provinces and I will not be able to send it to you earlier than in two weeks… Don't worry, I will take care of everything personally and you will have your certificate.

I think that my coming to America is impossible right now because I have no documents whatsoever. My "matura" and university diploma are all in Warsaw and mostly likely destroyed. But I am not thinking about it now. We are on the threshold of great events. I will write more detail in the letter that I send with your certificate.

Hugs,
Bolek

On March 28, 1940, Bolek fills out some more details of his life in Paris during the eerie period before the German invasion. A month later there is a sense of hopelessness while he waits to be drafted into the army.

April 13 and April 23, 1940

My dears,

I see from the last letter from Mikhal that slowly but gradually your life becomes more stable and that you are reaching clear waters. Unfortunately, I cannot say the same about us. The future looks foggy and uncertain. After a long harsh winter, the first rays of spring had an amazing charm for us. Trees started blooming, the air was filled with strange sweetness. I like this Paris spring and I am sure you remember it well. This time though, it is somewhat strange. There is fear in the air, uncertainty about the future, a strange anxiety which penetrates through all the gaps, and gnaws on one's heart. I live automatically. I try not to think about what will happen tomorrow.

Luckily I have some work and I manage somehow, even better than before. I changed the apartment and moved into a hotel wanting to use the pleasures of civilization like running water before I find myself in the circumstances when it will really be impossible. I would like to tell you that I am among the last ones who walk around Paris. Most of our colleagues are in the instruction camps of different formations of the army. You understand that making any plans to go to America is completely unrealistic right now. Besides I am a Polish citizen of a draft age and can't leave France.

I have to admit to you that I spend time quite pleasantly and that life in Paris goes on almost normally. Although we don't eat meat every day, and pastries are forbidden on certain days, as is alcohol. Recently there is gossip about the introduction of ration cards, but as you may guess, these are not the kind of things which would put me in a bad mood. I often think about my parents and ask myself with fear: How will they survive it!

My dears, I hope you get some news from your parents and as usual I believe in Mikhal's star. I am convinced that he passed his exams and that soon you will start normal life. Write to me often about your life, your friends. I am interested in everything. I keep saying it in every letter.

I hug you from the bottom of my heart, Bolek.

In case I should receive my draft card, your letters will be sent to the appropriate address.

And finally the last letter dated July 28, 1940, almost two and a half months after the invasion of France on May 10, 1940, and a month and a half after the armistice with Germany was signed on June 22, 1940. France was divided into an occupied zone in the north, including Paris as the capital and approximately two thirds of the territory of France, and an "independently governed" and unoccupied zone in the south, known throughout the war as Vichy because it was the capital. World War I war hero 84-year- old Marshall Philippe Petain was appointed as the president of what was known as the "free zone" or Vichy. The Vichy government in Southern France was controlled by a rightwing French government from 1940 to 1942. After 1942 and the Allied landings in North Africa, Vichy was reduced to a puppet regime.

In this letter Bolek describes a frightening escape from the army as the Germans approached his unit. My parents didn't hear from him again until the war ended.

Agen, July 28, 1940

My dears,

I would like to describe in a few words everything that happened to me recently. Naturally, I could make an entire epic of it. I was in the Polish army as a soldier. Germans were approaching and were ten kilometers from us. I threw my gun and the uniform in a ditch and started my journey. After indescribable obstacles, I traveled 300 kilometers to get to this town, of whose existence I had no idea. I was travelling for two weeks, without changing clothes, living on bread and water. I was walking countless kilometers, falling from exhaustion. Sometimes escapees in cars would help me pass tens of kilometers, and in this way I made it to Agen.[10] I was bombed three times on my way. I was lying in ditches for hours. I had moments when I thought, I didn't want to live, and I would lie in the ditch waiting for death. But my instinct kept pushing me forward and forward until I got to this town, which is located in a non-occupied zone.

They took me to the hospital for the escapees a center for refugees. They gave me food and they let me sleep. I was given a bed and bedding so I could rest a little. The food is very bad. Twice a day soup with bread, meat twice a week. I don't have any work. There are mainly old people, refugees tired of their journey. I have a few wounds and scratches, although this is not the worst. At least I have a roof over my head and food. Unfortunately, this hospital will soon close.

I came to Agen almost without clothing, in one shirt and a pair of shredded shoes. I had 50 francs in my pocket. Merciful hearts clothed me somehow. I got old clothing and two shirts and somehow I keep myself clean. I don't have any news from any of my friends. I don't know what happened to them. I am completely alone. I feel like a mouse in a trap; there is nowhere to escape. All the borders are closed, all exits barricaded. What will happen later? What will happen to me? I don't know what to ask you for. I would like to leave this accursed Europe, but how? How often I remember you and I ask myself if we will ever meet again in our life. Sometimes I think this is my end, that everything is over already. Perhaps I could go back to Paris, but I think it is too risky. And besides, what will I do there. Persecution of foreigners has already begun. Soon they will start with the Jews. No news from my parents.

When you have a chance, write to your parents that you got a letter from me. I suppose they are in touch with my parents. I don't even know their address. I can't write about it anymore. I wait impatiently for your letter. I am spending my last money on airmail.

I hug you strongly and wait for your response,
Bolek

The address where you can always write even if I move: Dr. B. Bejslechem, Hospital St. Marthe, Course Belgique, Agen (Lot et Garonne)
I am sorry for the tone of my letter, but trust me, it's not all. I left Paris on June 6ᵗʰ. I include a letter for Rosa.

France at the moment of the German invasion was not sufficiently prepared. Its energies for warfare had been sapped by the terrible toll taken on France in World War I and "and by a pacifism rooted in exhaustion, in deep pessimism (or realism) about whether France could survive another blood-letting on the scale of the Great War."[11]

Almost immediately after the German invasion a great "exodus" of the French population began fleeing from the North to the South. The road going south was crowded with desperate people. A report from a soldier whose unit was retreating described the evacuation this way:

People are thronging the roads, panic stricken…. The women, the kids, the old, lug trunks, suitcases, bundles, wheelbarrows, carts…. We try to chat with the civilians and immediately we understand.

The people are half mad, they don't even reply to what we ask them. There is only one word in their mouth: evacuation, evacuation.[12]

Some remembered atrocities from World War I and the effects of bombing. For Bolek being a foreigner, speaking French with an accent, and being Jewish certainly heightened his fears. At this point the thought of being a German prisoner of war would have been terrifying to any Jewish citizen, let alone a Jewish Pole from a conquered state where Germany had already implemented its racist ideology.

After the Armistice, all cities over 20,000 in population were considered open to those fleeing the German occupation in the North. This may explain the kindness of strangers that Bolek experienced when he reached Agen. Bolek did return to Paris after his escape.

In November, Ignace Schwarz, the friend of both Bolek and my father, writes to my parents. Ignace fled from Paris to the province, Hautes Pyrénées, that bordered Spain, a neutral country during the war. According to Ignace who learned this from mutual friends, Bolek had been in Paris for three months, which suggests that he left Agen very shortly after his escape from the army. He also describes Bolek as being desperate for assistance to leave France.

November 12, 1940

My Dear Mikhal and Hala,

This note must come as a surprise to you. Coming from a place you've certainly never heard of, you must be asking yourself, what sudden idea made me write to you?

It's quite simple. First, it's that I have never forgotten you. Second, I must bring to your attention the situation of our mutual friend Bolek, living in Paris at this moment, reduced to great disappointment.

Back in June, he had gone to join the Polish Army in France, as he had been ordered to do. In the meantime, there was "le débacle" [defeat] in France. Obliged to flee, he made it to Agen in the South of France, where he worked for a time in a hospital for refugees. Back in Paris for three months now, he is unemployed, without friends, living in poverty. It is Lucy [a friend of both Ignace and Bolek] who is living there who let me know about his situation by way of a gentleman who just arrived here because it's impossible to send mail between the two zones.

How did I get here? It's because of the circumstances. Called up to the Army at the beginning of March, I left for the front at the beginning of June. I followed the Army of the Loire in its defeat. Demobilized on September 1, ready to go back to work, they told me that because of my origin [his status as a Jewish foreigner] I could not cross the dividing line between the two Zones. Thankfully I found a friend who lives in Ibos, near Tarbes,[13] who was willing to take me in. In spite of unemployment here, I was able to find work in factory as a painter. Badly paid, just enough to live on.

Write me as soon as possible. What luck you had to cross the "herring pond"! The world is churning. Where will the waves throw us.

I shake your hands, both of you, in friendship,
Ignace.

Another letter arrives from Ignace, not dated but clearly written at roughly the same time:

I received a little card from Paris about Bolek. He really has things to complain about. Out of work, without even the right to think about work of any sort, he must be able to leave for America. If you think it's possible for you to get the money he'll need for it, send it to my address. In any case, as soon as possible, get in touch with me. I'll always be able to get in touch with him.

I think I'll be staying here at least for the winter, so you don't have to worry about how long your responses take. As for me, I am here without a single friend. Lucy will soon be leaving for Vichy, from where she will be able to come and join me. Thus he'll be all alone poor boy.

I'm so sorry,
Yours Ignace

I don't know what happened to Ignace, but I have photos of him in Paris playing cards with my father and other friends. In one of his previous letters Bolek describes Ignace as following his usual routine of "women and cooking." He was clearly the fun-loving bon vivant in my father's and Bolek's circle. Despite the differences among this circle of friends—in nationality and personality— they cared deeply for one another and were open in expressing these feelings.

In May 1941, the following postcard to my father comes from a woman named Raya Atlasberg regarding Bolek.

> *Dear Mr. Wolkowicz,*
>
> *I just received a letter from my sister who left Paris and now is in the unoccupied part of France. She has a message from Bolek Bejslechem (30 Rue Bernardin, Paris) for you. He asks you to try and get a visa, send money and write a letter. As there is no direct communication with Paris you can send a letter to my sister's address and she will send this to him. Her address is: Sonia Goldin, 37 Rue Beaupeyras, Clermont-Ferrand, France. Do not hesitate to use my sister as a connection. She will be glad to be helpful.*
>
> *Yours truly,*
> *R Altlasberg*

This message reveals Bolek's desperation. By this time, Paris was under Nazi control and there was nothing my parents could have done to help him. In June of that year, Germany invaded the Soviet Union, and in December 1941 the U.S declared war on Germany. Most likely my parents did not learn whether or not Bolek survived the war until August 1944 when France signed an Armistice with Germany.

I don't know how Bolek survived the war. Of the 350,000 Jews living in France before the war, less than half of them had French citizenship. About 200,000 of the foreign Jews lived in Paris and its outskirts. Some managed to find refuge in the countryside and also in Spain, which as a neutral country allowed Jews to use their country as a temporary escape route.

Once Bolek arrived in Paris he would have been subjected to a series of ordinances ordered by the police. A Nazi ordinance of September 21, 1940, forced Jews in the occupied zone to declare themselves as such at a police station. Encompassing Paris and its immediate suburbs, 150,000 people presented themselves at police stations. This information was then classified based on Jews of French nationality and foreign born Jews whose files were *in* different colors. The files were also classified by profession, nationality, and street. These files were handed over to the head of the Gestapo in France and used in various raids resulting in the deportation of Jews later during the war. I do not know whether or not Bolek declared himself at a police station, or if he found refuge, perhaps outside of Paris, and evaded this order.

A second ordinance in October 1940 proscribed various business activities for Jews, which probably accounts for Bolek being unemployed. In October1941, Jews were prohibited from owning radios all were confiscated forbidden to use public phones, to change their address or to leave their homes between 8 p.m. and 5 a.m. All public parks, places, theaters, and certain shops were closed to Jews. On the Metro they had to sit in the last car.

Beginning on May 14, 1941, there were several round- ups mainly of foreign Jews, ending in August, which involved both French and foreign Jews, most sent to Drancy, one of the main transit camps in France before deportation to concentration camps. Then again in May 1942, Jews were ordered to wear the yellow star; shortly thereafter on May 29,1942, the Nazis ordered a round-up of Jews, most of the them foreigners 13,000, including 4,000 children, on orders of the Vichy government to be delivered for deportation. First, they were herded into the cycling stadium Vel' d'Hiv and held there for several days without food, water, or sanitary facilities. The survivors were sent by train to Drancy in such horrific circumstances that many died en route. From there, a temporary holding place, they were transported to Auschwitz to be gassed.

Throughout the war, over 76,000 Jews were deported with the complicity of the police and the French railroad. Of the total of 76,000 who were deported, 50,000 Jews were deported from Paris, most foreign born; 13,000 were French citizens; the rest were immigrant Jews.[14] Another 14,000 died in French concentration camps for a total of 90,000 deaths, or slightly under a quarter of all French Jews.[15]

The French government made no acknowledgment of the complicity of the police and railroads in these deportations until 1995 when President Jacques Chirac offered an official apology and condemnation of the French police and national railroad that coordinated and supported these deportations and exceeded the quotas demanded by Germany.

At the same time, France had the third highest number of people who were commemorated for saving Jews by the Yad Vashem museum. France had fewer deportations based on the percentage of its population than other countries such as the Netherlands, where 75 percent of Jews were deported, or Belgium where 50 percent were deported. In a review of *Persecutions and Mutual Help in Occupied France: How 75 percent of the Jews of France Escaped Death* by Jacques Semelin, Robert Paxton[16] disagrees that France did its best to protect Jews. Paxton argues that only after 1942 did individual and group actions to save Jews, especially children, become widespread. Before then he stresses the complicity both of the Vichy government and the majority of French people in supporting Nazi orders, and even exceeding them, both in Occupied France and in Vichy France. For example, the Vichy government requested the deportation of more Jews in

May 1942 than requested by Nazi officials and also ordered the deportation of children, which the Gestapo had not requested.

In *When Paris Went Dark*, Robert C. Rosbottom makes a similar argument to Paxton's regarding the fate of Paris Jews. The book presents evidence that the Germans could not have succeeded as well as they did in rounding up illegals "if it had not been with the help of the local police force. The Germans quite simply did not have enough personnel to track and keep files on Jews or plan and carry out raids, arrests, and incarcerations. Nor did they know as intimately the labyrinth that was the city of Paris."[17]

To survive, Bolek must have had support from others. Perhaps he fled to the countryside surrounding Paris and was able to evade the authorities. He did survive, as did Toshka, and they may have married during the war. What I do know is that his survival was not possible without the collaboration of others.

Part II: Post-War Hopes—September 1945–April 1946

Bolek reconnected with my parents after the war. The three letters he sent them were written almost a year after the war in France ended and do not describe how he survived. The hardships of the war years are not mentioned, nor are the losses of loved ones.

The emphasis on day-to-day life is characteristic of survivors. They moved on. And yet they were victims of trauma, and the trauma returned in ways that were perhaps not understandable even to themselves. This is evident in the last letter from Bolek in 1946 when he finally shows anger at his one surviving uncle in New York City who has done nothing to help him. He is no longer able to contain his anger about the lack of understanding of what happened.

Eva Hoffman, whose parents were hidden in Poland during the war, discusses the psychological literature on such survivors and on their children born after the war. In *After Such Knowledge: Memory, History, and the Legacy of the Holocaust*, she says of the survivors' generation:

> In the unhappy typology of large-scale violence, genocide is the most uniquely unredeemed and dehumanizing, so radically repugnant as to tax the powers of language and of thought. It is the most extreme form of what Primo Levi called "gratuitous violence" — that is, violence directed not to the ends of battle or of victory but purely to the identity and existence of a targeted group. By now we know that among the most painful elements poured so venomously into

the victim's soul is precisely, the sense of humiliation not for having done anything, but for having submitted to degrading treatment. They were assaulted not for reasons of state, or as enemy combatants, but simply because of who they were. There is no framing that in any meaningful structure, and no meaningful action through which they could respond.[18]

I can imagine the sense of helplessness that the situation of enforced "victimhood" created, combined with a constant need to be on guard and protect oneself from being the next victim. This is not a memory that one wants to keep, and yet one does.

The two letters below describe Bolek's circumstances one year after the war ended. At the time of the correspondence with Bolek, my father, serving as a physician in the U.S. Army, my mother, and I (aged 3) were living on an Army base in Colorado Springs.

It is clear that Bolek would prefer to live in any other place than France. Even the Soviet Union is mentioned as a possibility since Toshka is from Lvov. The letters must also be understood in the context of the moment. France was liberated by the Allies in August 1944, but the economy was devastated, and there were still tremendous shortages of everything in 1945. Bolek thanks my parents for packages they have sent and talks about the circumstances of their lives. The optimism from before the war, and the passionate love affair have no place after the debacle of World War II. However, Bolek's gift for friendship is as evident as before the war. He also holds a guarded hope that he might be able to emigrate to the U.S.

Paris, 29 September, 1945

My Dears,

It brings me such pleasure to receive letters from you. I always find tokens of true friendship in them, an echo of by-gone years and a certain warmth which moves me time and again.

I would like to write to you about everything now, about what worries me and about problems which bother me the most. As I have already written you before, I work in OSE. It is a Jewish institution which has a few dispensaries available for the Jewish population. I work in one of them. It is quite well equipped. We possess a radio, diathermy, ultraviolet. On behalf of this dispensary, I make quite a few calls in town. Truth be told, it is not a fabulous job but it gives me partial satisfaction. My wife has so far earned a diploma "d'etudes superiors de Francais"[19] *and she presently works in an ofiice representing the association of Jews from Poland. I guess that you would want to know a few details, if I remember correctly, you were always curious as to what Bolek's wife would look like. I can tell you that we are very happy. Toshka is full of freshness and in part childlike enthusiasm, which is characteristic to people who are unspoiled by life. She's energetic, in telligent, capable of reaching ecstasy whenever she likes something, and she has her own character and her own personality which is difierent than mine. Most of all she adores theatre, poetry, books and cinema. In what I wrote, you certainly would be able to find some similarities with my character but despite that we difier in various respects. But I cannot write so much about it. I keep on thinking that we will meet again in life, that maybe you will come to Paris to visit… I smile at the very thought of it.*

We have for sure all changed. Conditions, surroundings, years have all left their marks but I am sure that we would be able to find each other again. And so life keeps on going further and further.

But it is so nice that we can stay in touch, and that our friendship keeps lasting. The pact into which we entered remains unbroken though life pushed us in difierent directions, and our fate sent us onto difierent roads; it is so pleasant that so many things join and unify us. But I can see that I strayed quite far from the topic and from what I wanted to write.

What do I intend to do? Recently I wrote that I would like to stay in France, but as of now it is quite difiicult, not many things have changed here and we encounter the same difiiculties as before the war. Now we are waiting for the elections, in any case this is a story quite long, I think, and one shouldn't really count on it. France is a country quite thankless towards foreigners. I don't include Poland in my plans for the reasons quite known to you, I am sure. I could also decide to go to Russia, Toshka is from Lvov and she could become a Soviet citizen. There also remains America, but I am aware that one needs to have quite a bit of money to even undertake such an endeavor, and there is also an issue of the 2-3 years which one needs to survive before one's diploma is legally recognized. I would like to know what you think about it and your opinion on this matter. So far, I cannot make a decision and I need to wait a little longer.

As of now I have received one letter from my uncle.

I am sending you his address, just in case you would happen to be in New York. It would be quite desirable if you could stop by at his place:

Max Wallace
3280 Rochambeau Ave
New York, Bronx 67

If you could talk to him a lot of things could get clarified because he didn't even mention it in his letter (my coming to America). You wrote me in your last letter that you found your cousin Adek.[20] Naturally, I know and remember him well. I recently received news from my friend, a doctor from Łódź who left just a month ago. I couldn't find any of our old friends. Everything has changed. And if I left today for Łódź, I would meander quite lonely among strangers. Jerzyk[21] Wiór wrote me a letter from Canada. I have a feeling that he is going to be doing quite well there.

My dears, we would like to thank you very much for the package, I assume that we will receive it soon. Dear Hala, we thank you very much for the trouble of sending a package to us. You ask what we need the most. Naturally, food still continues to be a problem for us, but things we need the most are underwear and clothing, as I mentioned to you in my last letter. Cofiee here isn't the expensive merchandise you imagine (at least at the moment). Since the Americans have arrived its price has fallen considerably. Cigarettes would bring us a lot of pleasure as both Toshka and I smoke. Apropos, Toshka is more or less Hala's height. She is maybe a little thinner.

We are also anxiously awaiting your photographs. Ours will be ready in ten days and I will send them in special mail. I will finish my long letter now, and I hope that it explains to you all about us.

Please write to us about yourself. We are interested in everything, your friends and neighbors, your work, your impressions, your daughter... in other words — everything.

I hug you tightly,
Bolek

I would very much like to meet you. Bolek has told me a lot about you. I am sending you my warmest greetings,
Toshka

Paris, 31 December, 1945

My Dears,

Please forgive a certain delay of my letters but a whole slew of circumstances contributed to it. First things first, I wanted to send you our photographs and I had to wait quite a bit for them. Toshka didn't come out quite well. She has a strange facial expression and I think that in real life she makes a much better impression. Besides that, I am quite a bit busier nowadays. I have quite a few calls downtown. We have a small flu epidemic here, and Toshka and I were its victims as well. I can't recall if I wrote to you already that we received your package. We thank you for all the special treats. They are still rarities here and they brought us a lot of pleasure.

I have greetings for you from Bollak and Delthilowa.[22] He changed beyond recognition, he grew oldand, literally, melted. She keeps herself quite well. She didn't grow older, bleaches her hair and, generally, she changed very little. Recently, when I was coming back from work, I met our old Mojżesz Michnik on rue du Temple.[23] We were both very happy. I visited him at home. He has a four-year-old son, his wife works as a seamstress and he has something to do with "maroquinier" [leather goods]. We talked about the old times and we were bringing back the years past, our buddies, acquaintances, and best friends. Mojżesz was asking a lot about you and he is going to write you a letter. He took your address from me. Recently, I also got a letter from my uncle which, I think, is fabulous for me.

He wrote to me that he got a letter from my friend, Dr. Wołkowicz, and that he and his wife are going to do everything in their power to help us come to the United States. He asked for a precise spelling of my last name so that he can apply for the afiidavit.[24]

Dear Michał, I thank you many times for putting your whole heart into arranging this matter. I have deep trust in your friendship and I know that you will not let me down. I am awfully curious about what you had written to him in your letter. Recently you wrote me that legalizing my diploma should take about three years. This point makes me uneasy. Especially since I haven't the slightest information about the financial capability of my uncle. I don't even know what he does for a living. It is a fact that he never himself ofiered to bring me to America. This all makes me think.

I have to add that for the last 6 months I got one packa ge and three letters. Despite this all, I think that coming to America is a good option for me. I count on myself, on my uncle, and of course, on you all. I know that you will do anything you can to make the matter move forward and that is why I start arranging things on my end full of energy. In France, very little has changed and there are few prospects for the future. I submitted my request for naturalization. It doesn't hurt to try. You ask how much I make, more or less. I make between 7 to 8 thousand a month. Toshka makes 4 thousand. It all sufiices to make a good living, but nothing more. I pay 1,500 francs a month for the apartment.

Meat costs about 150 francs per kilogram with ration cards, it's 300 francs on the black market. Cigarettes are 30 francs with ration cards and 110 francs otherwise. Everything is unbelievably expensive. After the first of January we will have ration cards for bread again. As you can see, life isn't too rosy.

I often think of the old years, my thoughts go back to the times when we were so alive and full of youthful zest, when we were high with our own ideas. High school, professors, love afiairs, flirts, parents, straight streets we knew so well. That world has collapsed and it would never come back. I recall Asnyk's[25] words:

"You have to go ahead with the living And not with wilted laurel leaves"

So I am going to go ahead because such is the law of life and it shouldn't be difierently...

My dears, I notice that I enter the route taking me away from reality, but whenever I write to you, I let myself be swept by thoughts and I often drift away...

I will end here. I hug you closely as your friend,
Bolek

Toshka is sending her warmest greetings to you.

Paris, April 2, 1946

My Dears,

I have received your letter and I want to thank you for all the trouble you had with the packages for me. My uncle and I would very much like for this letter to reach you before you leave for New York. I have very little time before the post leaves and that's why this letter will be seriously shortened. I will amend it another time and I will write more about many of us. I am very bitter as far as my uncle is concerned. I haven't heard from him at all for four months. Last time he wrote to me, he said that he was going to send me clothes. I even sent him my measurements but that was really the end of it.

Although I never asked him for anything he must understand that our life here isn't that easy. We live in a hotel and if I just had a little money I could find something else. Now the summer is coming, and anymore I don't remember how long it was since we went to the country last. Toshka looks bad and lost some weight. It would do us a lot of good if we could relax a little. What I make is enough to make a living but I cannot aford any extras. If I just had a little money, I could breathe easier.

Please let him know about all that because my pride doesn't allow me to write everything. Everyone with whomever I talk is outraged. It is truly unheard of. After the tragedy we all have been through, after the catastrophe which reduced all our family to just him and me. But perhaps all my broodings are false. Sometimes I think that perhaps he is poor and he cannot really help me. I hope that after your stay in New York some light will be shed on the matter. As for the afiidavit, I would like to have it just in case. I submitted my naturalization paperwork and I think that I might get lucky. If not, I would like to have America as security.

I will finish this chaotic letter but I would like you to be able to explain to me, as a consequence, if he could send me some money. It will bring me a great relief.

Please, also tell him that I would like to have the afiidavit just in case I wouldn't be able to settle in France.

I hug you warmly and I will write you more calmly and comprehensively as soon as I get the news from you.

Your friend,
Bolek

Adam Asnyk, whom Bolek quotes in his December 1945 letter, was a Polish poet forced to flee his homeland after participating in the 1863 uprising for the liberation of Poland from Russia. He fled to Galicia in the Austro- Hungarian Empire. His book of 30 sonnets, titled *Over the Depths*, was one of the best known books of Polish poetry. In it, he speaks of the struggle for survival as one of mutual interdependence and cooperation among communities, a spiritual rebirth. I think it is this that crosses Bolek's mind when he quotes the poem the need to shed "wilted laurels" but as a result to be reborn spiritually, to be renewed in a welcoming community. At the same time, it is clear from Bolek's letters that he is struggling. France would not be the country of his choice in which to live after all that has happened.

The difficult texture of Bolek's life comes through in his last letter to my parents in April 1946 scraping by, living in a hotel, having no money for clothes, a vacation or pleasure. And he expresses his exasperation and anger with his uncle, his only living relative, who made no effort to assist him in obtaining a visa to the U.S.

While the first two letters describe his efforts to move on a new love, marriage, work, and modest earnings this is clearly not enough. He feels trapped in a country that betrayed him, and his anger at his one living relative erupts in his last letter. The impossibility of "not remembering" must have haunted him. At the end of their lives, perhaps these memories, the impossibility of shedding "wilted laurel leaves" may have fueled Bolek's and Toshka's decision to commit suicide together. Neither wanted to live alone with their memories of the war years. Together they had created something new — a life together, and raising a wonderful and successful adopted son, now a man. Perhaps the thought of being alone with painful memories was not bearable.

A poem by Dan Pagis, "Instructions for Crossing the Border,"[26] speaks to the dilemma of survivors such as Bolek and Toshka: the attempt at "not remembering" and creating new lives, but also failing at "not remembering." The final lines of the poem speak to the dilemma: "You are not allowed to forget."

> Imaginary man, go. Here is your passport.
> You are not allowed to remember.
> You have to match the description:
> Your eyes are blue.
> Don't escape with the sparks
> Inside the smokestack:

you are a man, you sit in the train.
Sit comfortably.
You've got a decent coat now,
a repaired body, a new name
ready in your throat
Go. You are not allowed to forget.

Bolek and Toshka, 1945

Endnotes

1 Boleslaw Bejslechem (pronounced Belem), with an accent on the last syllable. Bolek is a nickname for Boleslaw. It is the name he always used.

2 I imagine that Bolek and Rose communicated in Yiddish since she did not speak French and he did not speak English.

3 Approximately $57. To put this in perspective, a well-paid worker in an armaments factory made this amount in one week.

4 A close friend of both Bolek and my father who survived the war. I also met him on the 1955 trip to France.

5 His parents, like my grandparents lived in Lodz. But by this time Lodz was occupied by the Germans, and Jewish families were being displaced from their homes and fleeing from one apartment to another, and, if they could, to other cities, mainly Warsaw.

6 Bolek is referring to documents regarding my father's French medical degrees that he needed to establish himself as a physician in the U.S.

7 Ignace Schwarz was Bolek's and my father's friend from Paris.

8 A mutual friend from Poland, Moishe or Moses Michnik, mentioned in the letter to my parents dated October 13, 1939.

9 Riga was then part of the Soviet Union as a result of the Hitler/Stalin Pact of August 1939. The pact kept the Soviet Union temporarily out of the war and gave over vast parts of Poland's territory to the Soviet Union that formerly belonged to Poland.

10 Agen is a small town in the Southern part of France between Toulouse and Bordeaux in the province of Lot Garonne.

11 Jackson, *The Fall of France: the Nazi Invasion of 1940*, 149.

12 Ibid, 176.

13 Tarbes is a French commune in the Haute Pyrénées in France. This region borders Spain.

14 These figures are based on Robert Paxton's seminal work, *Vichy France: Old Guard and New Order*. See also Renee Poznanski, *To Be a Jew in France 1939–1945*.

15 Estimates differ on the exact number of Jews who died. Serge Klarsfeld concluded that 77,500 died in concentration camps or were shot thus slightly less than a quarter of the population. Serge and Beate Klarsfeld are activists who documented the Holocaust to enable prosecution for war crimes.

16 Paxton, *New York Review of Books*, March 6, 2014.

17 Rosbottom, *When Paris Went Dark*, 257.

18 Hoffman, 43-44.

19 French Diploma of Higher Education

20 My father's first cousin who survived the war in the Soviet Union.

21 Jerzyk is diminutive for Jerzy; George in English.

22 Delthilowa is the last name of a woman married to a man named Delthil.

23 Rue du Temple is the main street in the Marais, the historic Jewish quarter in Paris.

24 "Affidavit" also known as Immigration and Naturalization Form I-134, Affidavit of Support.

25 Adam Asnyk, a well-known Polish poet and writer (1838- 1897).

26 In Langer, *Art From the Ashes*, 591.

Chapter 7

The Survivors Dosia and Adek

After the War: 1945–47

From 1943 to 1947, my mother and I accompanied my father as he moved from one army assignment to another Muskogee, Oklahoma; Colorado Springs; and Fort Leavenworth and Fort Riley, Kansas. He was a physician in the United States Army then, and his assignments depended on where an ophthalmologist was most needed. He was honorably discharged from the army in 1947. We piled our belongings into our two-door Chevy, said good bye to friends, and drove across the United States in August at the peak of the summer heat. After a week we arrived in Philadelphia, where I was born, and where my father had previously practiced medicine. I was five years old.

Entering Philadelphia, we drove down the avenue that runs alongside the port. A giant grain elevator loomed. We passed docks, barges, and deserted piers, finally arriving at a cobblestone street with the number 15 trolley clanging down the center. Small brick row houses lined each side of the street. Our house, only a short distance from the port of Philadelphia, was a narrow three-story brick building, with two steps leading to the front door, much like most of the other houses. A grocery store across the street sold delicious rye bread, and a bar on the corner was always busy, day and night.

My parents had hired people to repair, paint, and clean our house, and arranged for our furniture to be moved back after the renters left. I had no memory of this place since I was only one when we left, but I immediately liked our two floors located directly above my father's office. It meant that my father was nearby most of each day.

Our return, however, was overshadowed by two events. First, my mother had to be hospitalized right after we arrived. She had sustained a serious injury before we left Fort Riley that required hospitalization. While horseback riding, which she did with my father, she was thrown and her left arm splintered in many places. When we arrived in Philadelphia her arm was encased in a heavy shoulder to fingers cast. She was immediately admitted for surgery at Temple University Hospital.

My father had to resume his practice. From the day he opened his office, there were more patients than he could handle, and the waiting room was always overflowing. My mother was not alright. The bones in her arm were not mending and the surgery she required consisted of several operations to prevent an amputation. The hospital was far from where we lived, and children were allowed limited access to patients. I felt bereft no mother, an unfamiliar city and home, my father constantly at work.

Shortly after we arrived, and while my mother was in the hospital, Dosia, my father's first cousin who had survived the war, came to stay with us. Dosia, who spoke little English, lay on our green velvet couch most of the day smoking Lucky Strikes and listening to the radio the sounds of "I'm Looking Over a Four-Leaf Clover" and "Goodnight Irene" soothing her. She was 23 years old.

Her lassitude silently expressed her suffering. She tried to help my father by offering to take care of me, but I stubbornly refused. Once she attempted to help me with my bath, but I angrily shut the bathroom door and locked it. I was a five-year-old in desperate need of my mother, in a new city, with a father working around the clock to reestablish his practice. At one point, I hurled myself down the stairs, hoping that I too would break a bone and join my mother in the hospital.

That Dosia came to us deeply traumatized, a survivor of the war and of Auschwitz was not something a five-year-old could have understood. She and I got off to a very difficult start that summer. For each of us the memories remained painful.

After the war, while she and her brother Adek were in a Displaced Persons Camp in Germany, Dosia had married a man considerably older than she was. She emigrated to the States first, with her husband planning to join her shortly afterwards. While staying with us, she and her U.S. immigration lawyer fell in love. Dosia acknowledged to my father that her marriage was not based on love.

My father tried to convince her to follow her heart, leave her husband, and marry the man she loved. But she was too frightened to lose the security that her husband's financial support provided. He had succeeded in making money on the black market and supported her generously. She broke off the love affair and rejoined her husband when he came to the States.

My Father's Cousins: Dosia and Adek

Dosia and Adek were both considerably younger than their cousin, my father twelve and nine years respectively. My father left Poland to attend the university in Grenoble at the age of 20 when they were still children. He was someone they looked up to, and after the war saw as the head of the family that remained. Dosia and Adek also had a younger sister, Dzjunia, who died in Auschwitz along with their parents.

Growing up, my father and later Adek went to the same school in Lodz, a progressive one that offered a rigorous curriculum in Polish and modern Hebrew. It is possible that Dosia also attended this school, as there were separate schools for girls and boys run by the same organization, known as Tarbut Schools. An outstanding student, Dosia was gifted in learning languages. Soon after she came to the States she spoke flawless English and later in life also became fluent in Italian.

When the war began, Dosia was 17 and Adek 20. According to a letter written by Dosia to my parents after the war, the family fled from Lodz, which was occupied by the Germans shortly after they invaded Poland, to Tomaszov Mazovieski, a town in the southeastern part of Poland.

Unlike Dosia, Adek fled to the Soviet Union, which was safer for Jews than Poland. I do not know where he spent the war years, but during this time, he fell in love with and married a woman named Ruchla (known as Ruth in the States). By the time Adek and Dosia contacted my parents after the war ended, he was married to Ruth and had returned to Lodz, working as a technician in an industrial company.

Photo of Adek, dated 10/6/29

The letter below, written by Adek, may have been the first letter my father received after the war in Europe ended on May 8, 1945, following the surrender of Germany. It may have been the first time that he and my mother learned definitively of their family's fates—that everyone died during the war except for Dosia and Adek.

Printed on top of the envelope:

Sender A.Wołkowicz
Łódź
Piłsudski Street 72, apartment 1
c/o Mr. Fiszman
Poland

Dosia (seated) and her sister, Lodz circa 1928. The only photo I have of Dosia as a child.

Addressee
Mr. Michail Love
Philadelphia
315 Pine Street
United States of North America
U.S.A.

Stamp
Checked by army censorship
Polish Post Ofiice
Warsaw — the capital, Odra and Nissa — borders[1]

Łódź, July 11th, 1945

My Dears,

I wrote to you many times from Russia, where my wife and I spent the entire war, but I didn't receive any answer from you. After returning home, I didn't find anybody from our family, except for my younger sister, Dosia. Everybody was murdered by Hitler's bandits. Dosia came back in a horrible state and she still is not well after a stay in the infamous death camp in Oświęcim,[2] which you must have heard of. Write to us how you are doing. Do you have children? Etc.

I would like to come to you, because, besides my wife, you are my only family who is still alive (I forgot about Szymek[3]). Here very sad memories haunt me wherever I go. If you could send me a package with clothing, I would really appreciate it.

I kiss you very tenderly and wish you all the happiness
Adek[4] with wife and Dosia

Dosia's letter followed in October, but apparently she had sent other letters which my parents had not received. Dosia, the more fluent writer, described her experiences during the war and the urgency she and Adek felt to leave Poland because of the "emptiness around them."

Łódź, October 5th, 1945

My dear Halinka and Michaś!

I am trying one more time to write to you and I hope that this time this letter will be delivered to you. Why haven't we received any answer to our letters and telegrams so far?

I am wondering how I should start this letter. Well, perhaps with words of consolation. I understand your pain very well, because I am going through exactly the same thing. I feel indescribably sorry that I have to be a messenger of such tragic news. As you have probably guessed, your dear parents perished. Unfortunately! Just as my parents, Dziunia[5], and my entire family they shared a tragic fate of millions of Jews. They fell victims to Hitler's bandits in the summer of 1942, during the "destruction of Jews"[6] which encompassed the entire Europe occupied by Germans.

**Letter from Dosia Wolkowicz after the war to my parents.
Dosia is my father's first cousin from his father's family.**

I was together with your parents, Michałek, till March of 1940. After compulsory leaving of their apartment at Gdańska Street, they moved in with us. When they organized a "ghetto" in Łódź, they escaped to Warsaw, we to Tomaszów. Unfortunately it turned out that there is no escape from Hitlerite barbarians. All of our family died a tragic death in gas chambers. I survived thanks to a miracle, or, if you like, destiny. After having gone through hell of concentration camps (among others, I was in the death camp in Oświęcim), I came back from Czechoslovakia, where I was working in an ammunition factory.[7] I came back to Łódź, falsely hoping that perhaps someone from our family is alive. But no such luck! The truth was tragic, for apart from Adek and his wife, who have been in the USSR since the outbreak of the war, nobody from our entire family was saved.

Adek and his wife took such great care of me and I owe him my life, because I came back from the camp in a state of complete exhaustion. Right now I work in the district administrative ofiice, and Adek is an inspector in the industrial board of directors. Our earnings are disproportionately small in comparison with the high prices of food products and clothing. But this wouldn't be the worst, for we are young, full of energy and feel the strength to build a new life. But not here!

We want to get out of here at any cost, because there are no possibilities for existence for us here. We are horrified by the emptiness surrounding us here, in the country where we experienced the happiest, but unfortunately, not to be repeated years, surrounded by the people who are dearest to us. Besides that, anti- Semitism is growing here with every day and the atmosphere is becoming unbearable. All the Jews want to leave and many left already. Our deepest wish is to also leave here as soon as possible.

We know very well that there is an opportunity togo to United States, because many of our friends already received the so called "afiidavit" from their cousins in America. So we turn to you with a great appeal that you would do everything in your power to make this leave possible for us. We hope that you will fulfill our plea and that you will start doing something in this direction. Especially, because all three of us are young and we will surely be able to take care of ourselves. After all, Adek has a great job, he is a textile technician and his wife is an unusually talented, intelligent and industrious woman. As far as I am concerned, I passed my "matura"[8] in 1939, I know a few foreign languages, and I was going to study medicine, but right now it's not possible.

My dears! Take our plea into your heart. We know that we will not be disappointed, because we are your only cousins, who remained alive, and knowing your attitude towards us we trust that you will do everything in your power to make our leave possible.

Our cousins from Paris, Dabek, are presently in New York. Their address: Dabek brothers 214 West 39th Street, New York City. Perhaps you could contact them.

I am finishing my long letter and I am asking for a fast reply. Write everything about yourselves.

I kiss you very warmly,
Your cousin Dosia.

Adek and his wife send kind regards. P.S.
I am writing below our exact birthdates, which will surely be necessary for our documents

Abram (Adek) Wolkowicz, born in Łódź, August 28th, 1919
Rena (Ruth) Wołkowicz, born in Warsaw, December 3rd, 1917
Dorota[9] (Dosia) Wołkowicz, born in Łódź, October 7th, 1922
We are sending a letter to Szymek Jofie as well. Most likely you are in touch with him. Send us their exact address.

In this letter Dosia reduces the four years of horror that she survived and the tragic deaths of her and my father's families to a brief narrative. The paucity of detail speaks more than a thousand words the crimes too great and too painful to be elaborated. To describe is to remember, to recall pain over and over. And perhaps for Dosia there were feelings of guilt as well "why me?" and not the others.

Her family's flight to the town of Tomaszov Mazovieski, situated in southeast Poland, was understandable. It was a town to which other Jews fled in the hope that it would provide refuge from the German occupation. Dosia's family fled in March 1940, before the ghetto was enclosed in Lodz in May of that year.

Before the war, Tomaszov was a town that included 10,000 Jews, approximately a third of the population, primarily merchants and artisans of various kinds and laborers in an artificial silk-making factory. Like other medium sized towns of this period, it had a vibrant political and intellectual life with the full range of Jewish schools from Orthodox to Zionist and Bundist and a Jewish "popular college" that provided lectures on many topics.

Because of the influx of Jews from Lodz and Warsaw after the onset of the war, the Jewish population grew from 10,000 to more than 15,000. A ghetto was established in the town in December 1940, soon after Dosia's family arrived. According to Dosia's letter, it was during the summer of 1942 that members of her family, other than herself, were transported to death camps. It is not clear how she survived.

If the family had stayed in Tomaszov they would have been deported in October 1942 when the Germans began their ruthless plan for deportation to gas chambers and selection of the able-bodied for labor. On October 28, Ukrainian, German, and Latvian police surrounded the ghetto and on October 31 rounded up the majority of Jews who were sent to death camps. Approximately 900 young people were left behind as were several hundred Jewish townspeople who were deemed useful labor.[10] From Dosia's description it seems that perhaps she was left behind as a worker while the rest of the family was deported to a death camp.

Although the chronology is unclear, it seems that Dosia was sent by the Nazis to several concentration camps after moving to Tomaszov and before being sent to work in an ammunitions plant in Czechoslovakia. Her final destination was Auschwitz, which she calls by its Polish name, Osvieciem.[11] the name of the town in which it was situated.

In the United States, Dosia told my parents about her imprisonment in Auschwitz II-Birkenau.[12] She told them that she had been selected to go to the gas chamber; however, she had been a worker before the selection was made, and on the way to the gas chamber slipped into a small locker, which she fit into because she was wasting away from hunger. Somehow she summoned the strength to return to work. I do not know whether she was among the 7000 prisoners who remained after the Soviet Army liberated the camp on January 27, 1945, or if she was among the 60,000 forced to a "death march" before the Allies entered. Of those forced to march, 15,000 died.

She recounted some aspects of her tragic story to my parents when she came to the U.S. in 1947, but I never learned the details, and it would not have occurred to me to ask. Indeed, my parents never mentioned Dosia's story to me again after the initial telling when I was old enough to understand.

Dosia's description of anti-Semitism in Lodz after the war shocked me. After reading about this period, I found that her description was amply documented. In addition to the well-known pogroms in both Krakow and Kielce, the latter during which more than 40 Jews were murdered in August 1946, Jan Gross's book, *Fear: Anti-Semitism in Poland After Auschwitz*, documents the history of Jewish oppression in the post-war years.

He describes the hostile reaction of many Poles immediately after the war to those Poles who had bravely saved children; in fact the "rescuers" were forced to hide their actions, and in many villages Jews who returned were threatened with death. After having been saved in a nearby village, a Jewish doctor who returned to Krakow, his home town, after the war reported:

> ....after I returned to Krakow, some 2-3 weeks following my departure from the village where I stayed last, it became known that I was a Jew. Already after this area got liberated, I was threatened there with death, and the good, innocent people who gave me shelter were threatened with flogging and having their house set on fire.[13]

This is a scenario that happened time and time again. The impetus being, according to Gross, not what was commonly thought the attribution of Communism to Jews who were numerous in the Party and held high-level positions. Rather, Gross describes the "widespread collusion in the Nazi-driven plunder, spoliation, and eventual murder of the Jews that generated Polish anti-Semitism after the war, not the alleged postwar Jewish collusion in the imposition of Communism in Poland."[14] Indeed, he describes the situation as being one in which the Communist Party ignored the plight of Jews in the post-war period so as to gain "legitimacy in the eyes of the Polish population, and adopted what at best can be described as an attitude of benign neglect in matters Jewish."[15]

Statistics as to the actual number of anti-Semitic incidents in post-war Poland vary. According to one study, which examined documents from the Polish Ministry of Public Administration, between September 1944 and September 1946 there were 130 incidents of anti-Semitism in 102 locations, in which 327 Jews lost their lives. The highest number of deaths in one place occurred in Kielce, a terrifying pogrom that occurred on July 4, 1946, in which 42 Jews were brutally murdered.[16] This pogrom, which occurred after Dosia and Adek left Poland, precipitated a major exodus of Jews from Poland.

In Lodz, 28 Jews died between November 1944 and December 1945. After the agonies of the war, the fear of being targeted by anti-Semites must have been unbearable for Jews returning to their homes. Poland was no longer a place in which Jews were welcome or felt safe. As Dosia put it: *We want to get out at any cost because there are no possibilities for us here.*

The final letter before emigrating came from Adek in October 1946. He and Dosia and his wife Ruth were now in a Displaced Persons Camp in Eschwegge, Germany, run by the United Nations Relief and Rehabilitation Administration (UNRRA), an international relief agency formed by 44 countries in 1943 to "plan, coordinate, administer or arrange for ….the relief of victims of war in any area under the control of the United Nations through provision of food, fuel, clothing, shelter and other basic necessities." The "United Nations" in the name refers to the countries that had agreed to fund and administer it. In the three years it operated in Germany to help displaced persons with housing, clothing, and food in order to get back on their feet, it distributed about four billion dollars worth of goods and services.[17]

> *Eschwege, April 22, 1946*
>
> *My Dears!*
>
> *I have yet to receive any replies to my letters to you or the Dabeks. We now live in UNRRA camp in the American Zone in Germany and we are waiting for the opportunity to emigrate. We have registered through "Joint"[18] in the American Consulate in Frankfurt am Main[19] (I sent our address to Philadelphia). However one needs to have an afiidavit from friends in America. Those who have the papers can go next month. If we receive the*

afiidavit then we would be able to emigrate, even this year. The number of emigrations is limited and many Jews have already received their papers. In Berlin, I have only received one letter from Bolek via Paris and Łódź.

I ask you to please write to the Dabeks so that together you could send us the afiidavits as soon as possible. Please send the original to the address of my sister in law in Paris, and send a copy to our address in Eschwege.

I also wrote to Szymek in Bremen but I didn't get any answer.

Is he still in the military?

And you have already been released from the military, right?

I send you my warmest kisses,

Adek

Greetings from my wife and sister.
The address in Paris:
Fernande (Frajda) Goldreich
51 rue d'Hauteville, Paris (10e)

Our address
D.P. Camp[20] UNRRA Team 522
Eschwege b/Kassel
Hessen Nassau Germany
Abram Wolkowicz
block 16/8

Our personal information:
Wolkowicz Abram born on August 22, 1912 in Łódź
Wolkowicz Ruchla born on December 3, 1916 in Warsaw
Wolkowicz Dorota born on October 7, 1922 in Łódź

Envelope:
D. P. Camp UNRRA Team 522
Eschweg b/Kassel
block 16/8

I do not know the circumstances under which Dosia and Adek gained a place in the Displaced Persons Camp awaiting affidavits that allowed them to emigrate to the United States. They did not arrive in the U.S until the summer of 1947 — what must have felt like an interminable wait. Two and a half years after the termination of the war, Dosia came to live with my parents and me. By this time, Dosia had become a very different person than the one she was in her 1945 post-war letter. In the letter she is devastated by her losses but still hopeful for a new life. By 1947, she had settled for a husband she did not love, was torn by a love for another man, and saw little happiness ahead of her.

New Lives, New Names

Dosia's husband finally joined her, as did Ruth, Adek's wife. One of the first steps they took was to change their names to non-Jewish names. Dosia's married name Luczanowski became Louis, and Adek and Ruth changed Wolkowicz, also my family name, to Walker.

The two couples decided to make their living as chicken farmers in Vineland, New Jersey. This location and plan was not a surprising choice. The original Jewish settlement in Vineland was sponsored by the Alliance Colony, an organization founded in the late nineteenth century by philanthropists in the United States to help provide a livelihood and home for Jews fleeing from the Russian pogroms at the end of the nineteenth century, Although this community no longer existed in the 1940s, Vineland was still viewed as a place where Jews lived and could farm in a safe environment.

Both couples bought chicken farms not very far from one another. I recollect very happy childhood visits to Adek's and Ruth's farm. By this time Adek and Ruth had a child named Arlene. I, at seven years old, and she a delightful child of two loved each other. I felt very grown up helping to care for her. Everything about the farm was wonderful and new to me the newly hatched chicks cared for in heated incubators, the hens sitting dutifully on their eggs, and the delicious meals that included farm eggs and occasionally a fresh killed chicken. It seemed idyllic. But what seemed a perfect setting to a seven-year-old was not what either family wanted.

Eventually, Adek left Vineland to fulfill the immigrant dream of seeking wealth in the West. He and his family settled in Los Angeles, where he and Ruth bought a liquor store and prospered. I never saw Adek again, although he and my father spoke from time to time, and I received a wedding invitation to Arlene's wedding but was not able to go. I was married and in graduate school by then and had not been in touch with Adek's family for many years.

Dosia and her husband moved to Manhattan on the Upper West Side where many Jewish Holocaust survivors settled. They lived among fellow refugees from Poland, including their French relatives, the Dabeks, whom Dosia mentions in her post-war correspondence. She and her husband were able to maintain a Polish/European way of life by staying mainly within this circle of friends and relatives. Dosia had a "nose job" so that she would not look Jewish and dressed fashionably. After trying for many years to become pregnant, she had a son, Daniel, who was the center of her life. He went to elite private schools, where he thrived academically, and then to Princeton where he became a pre-medical student.

Dosia's Tragic End

My father remained in constant touch with Dosia. As the years progressed, however, she grew increasingly depressed. She had never loved her husband and eventually decided to divorce him. While living alone she began to descend into a deep depression triggered by the need to replace her teeth with dentures. Her health, including her teeth and gums, had been neglected during the war, and eventually her teeth had to be extracted.

This reminder of the war years precipitated a nervous breakdown. Following the protocols of the time, Dosia agreed to and received shock treatments. But just as she seemed to emerge from the treatments, a final blow in her sad life destroyed her. During a trip home from Princeton, her son Daniel was killed in a car accident. Dosia, in indescribable grief, left the States, and moved to Lugano, Italy, where she learned Italian and lived out the rest of her life among a circle of retirees.

She visited me once when she returned to see friends in the States. By then she was an alcoholic and drug addict. She asked me for a drink shortly after she arrived. A half bottle of Southern Comfort was the only hard liquor I had in the house, and Dosia quickly downed it. After dinner I held her up as she wobbled to a waiting cab. I kissed and hugged her, but she was in her own world of sorrow and alcohol. It was the last time I saw her. Shortly after this sad evening, Adek called to tell me that she had died in Lugano.

The death of her son was the final blow. The company of people who saw her strengths and knew the tragedy of her life helped her survive for some time in Lugano. But in the end, the war took its final toll. She had no one left to love and live for.

Reflections on Dosia

My memory of Dosia when she first came to live with us is seared in my mind. Perhaps this is because it was a period of childhood sadness and pain for me, which Dosia could not have understood. I can easily imagine her distress that the only welcome to the U.S. was her beloved cousin, whom she longed to be with and who was working around the clock, and whose child rejected her attempt to be caring. Dosia also remembered this moment and always reminded me of it. I think that a rejection from anyone at that moment, even from a five-year-old, was too painful to bear.

When I became an adolescent and could begin to understand the meaning of what Dosia went through, I became fixated on the Holocaust. Because Dosia had survived, her suffering mattered much more to me than the deaths of my grandparents and other relatives, whom I never knew. Dosia, who lay on our green couch with a Band-aid covering the numbers on her arm embodied for me the enduring, underlying, and mostly hidden sadness in our family.

Dosia lived among other survivors, which must have been a relief no need to explain what happened. I wonder now what her life would have been like had she lived to tell her story publically, as some survivors eventually have, for example, for the Yale Testimony Project. I wonder if in the telling there would also have been some satisfaction because of the public recognition of what she and others suffered.

These are mere speculations, but Dosia, like so many other survivors, presented herself not only as someone who had moved on, but as someone who had literally reinvented herself. This was especially true of her appearance that of a glamorous and wealthy Upper West Side New Yorker. I believe that Dosia was all these things, as well as a loving mother and relative to my parents, especially to my father, whom she trusted and turned to before anyone else. But the Dosia who wrote the letter in 1945 with such clarity and hope for a future that she would create, with help from my parents, was gone.

This poem by Emily Dickinson touches on what may have been an essential psychological truth for Dosia and other Holocaust survivors:

> There is pain — so utter —
> It swallows substance up —
> Then covers the Abyss with — Trance
> So Memory can step
> Around — across — upon it — [21]

This is needed to live and move forward, however one does it—around, across, upon.

Similarly, Charlotte Delbo's words may express what Dosia felt as a survivor of Auschwitz: *I am not among the living. I died in Auschwitz and no one notices it.*[22]

Endnotes

1 These are the new borders of Poland favorable to the Soviet Union, which kept the areas it had occupied during the war. Odra is a river in the East, Nissa a river in the West. The eastern territories were acquired by the Soviet Union, and the western territories were expanded into what was previously Germany.

2 He is referring to Auschwitz which was located in the town of Oswiecim.

3 Nickname for Szymon; Simon in English. He was another cousin who emigrated to the United States before the war as a teenager. My parents eventually become good friends with him and his family.

4 Adek—short for Avram.

5 Nickname for her sister.

6 Dosia uses a term here which my translator was unable to identify, but she thinks the meaning is clear.

7 The sequence here is unclear. From her description it seems she was able to leave Auschwitz because she was sufficiently able-bodied to work in a munitions factory. Based on her account to my parents, which I use in my description, Auschwitz was her final destination and she survived until the camp was liberated. After the war ended Dosia returned to Lodz.

8 Equivalent to a high school diploma plus two years of college.

9 Dorothy, in English.

10 www.holocaustresearchproject.org/nazioccupation/tomas zow-mazowiecki.html

11 Auschwitz is the German name for this town where the two camps were located. Auschwitz I was the original camp erected in 1940-41, and construction began on Auschwitz II-Birkenau in 1941 to ease the overcrowding of the first camp and because it served the dual purpose of extermination as well as forced labor. The first gas sing facility began operating in March 1942.

12 Auschwitz-Birkenau II, approximately one kilometer from Auschwitz I, was both death camp and concentration camp with new capacity for gassing thousands in a day.

13 Gross, *Fear: Anti-Semitism in Poland after Auschwitz: An Essay on Historical Interpretation*, xi.

14 Ibid., xiv.

15 Ibid., xiv.

16 Ibid., 81-117.

17 https://en.wikipedia.org/wiki/United_Nations_Relief_and_ Rehabilitation_Administration

18 This refers to the Jewish Joint Distribution Organization which provided relief to Jews suffering from anti- Semitism

19 Frankfurt am Main is located in West Germany.

20 DP camp a Displaced Persons camp; a temporary facility for people who were forced to leave their homes during World War II.

21 Quoted in Hartman, *The Longest Shadow: In the Aftermath of the Holocaust*, 158.

Afterword — A Daughter's Reflections

As a child, I felt proud of my parents. They had pluck and stamina. When my parents left Uncle Love, they gave up the chance to inherit his practice and wealth. They moved to a Polish working class neighborhood, rented a house, and began to practice medicine in an office on the ground floor.

My father was immediately sought out as a physician— this despite the anti-Semitism that surfaced in our neighborhood. I have a letter that my father preserved. It was written when a colleague, Dr. Sklaroff, announced that he was leaving for the army and that my father, Dr. Michael Wolkowicz, would take over his practice in his absence. A rabid anti-Semite sent the announcement back, the envelope itself threatening, with its "Mr. and Mrs. Moishe Wolkowicz," and inside: *Listen you kike, why don't you go around your own kind instead of leading the Gentile people to think you are a Christian. Your (stet) a Dirty Jew. Your Still A Butcher.* My father kept it as reminder to me that anti-Semitism was not limited to Europe.

He was eager to join the United States Army but was rejected twice because he did not pass the physical. As a young man he had tuberculosis, and the scar tissue was still visible on an X-ray. The third time he applied he was accepted and enlisted in 1943. He wanted to be part of the fight against Nazi Germany and asked to go abroad but was instead sent to various bases around the country, and we went with him.

For my parents, being a part of the struggle against Nazism was important. It was also an introduction to this country's beauty as well as a lesson in its racism: segregated troops, inferior housing for African American soldiers, and the racism openly expressed by people around us. It was a lesson that profoundly affected my parents' understanding of and opposition to this country's continuing history of racism. It also affected how they raised me.

An important lesson occurred when I was five years old. In Fort Riley there was segregated housing, as on all army bases. In addition there was a shortage of housing, especially for African Americans. We had a spacious top floor that was unused, and my parents offered it to an African American family who had two boys, both a few years older than I was. I loved having these playmates, and my parents encouraged me to play with them. Women who lived near us took my mother aside, acknowledging that she as a foreigner did not know the "American way." They told her that I should not be playing with the boys. My mother ignored them, and I continued enjoying my older playmates. My parents' behavior in a number of situations throughout my childhood that involved race spoke louder than words.

When I was seven, my mother became pregnant and gave birth to a girl, who was named for my maternal grandmother, Mera Kagan Rozin. I never saw my sister, although she lived long enough to be named. She died in the hospital, her enlarged heart a result of my mother's preeclampsia. This loss brought back all that my parents lost before. As a child, I could not understand my parents' sadness about their losses. But when my sister died I had my own loss. I so wanted a sister or brother in our tiny family. The bassinet was already in my parents' bedroom, and a few baby clothes were placed in my room, which adjoined theirs. It was a shocking and sad moment in our family that like the many losses in the past went unspoken. However, at least I knew her name Miriam.

Her death was a turning point for me as a child. I became much more independent, often not talking with my parents about what happened in school. I made my friends an important part of my life. The silence in our family about loss and the closing of doors to the past deeply affected all of us.

In spite of their losses, my parents made many lifelong friends, including several in the army. I still have a cookbook that one of their army friends, Lola Gordon, co-produced with other women from Hadassah. My husband still makes Lola's chocolate roll. My parents entertained often and when I was young loved to dance. I have their Polish tango records, which they put on when their close friends from Poland and France visited. My father was a joke teller, and in his organized way collected jokes so he would be ready with them when he was with friends. Sometimes his punctiliousness about table manners (he would never touch cooked food, such as a chicken bone, with his hands) a residue of his mother's upbringing made my mother and me laugh until we cried.

As a child my parents told me many stories about their lives in Poland and France. Despite these stories, I also felt their unexpressed taboo about asking more than I was told. I also experienced the enactment of the "taboo" in 1981 when I went to Poland with my husband who was invited to attend an international conference there in his field of fluid mechanics. In Warsaw, we stayed with my husband's colleague, who was a leader in the Solidarity Movement and whose wife, then deceased, was Jewish. His adult children, who self-identified as Jews, gladly took us around "Jewish" Warsaw, of which very little remained or was at that time memorialized. Poland, however, was experiencing an interesting moment. Lech Walesa had emerged as a leader of Solidarity. The atmosphere in Warsaw was charged with hope for change. Although food was scarce, with nothing in the stores except potatoes, rye bread, sausage, and apples, the exhilaration of replacing an oppressive regime was in the air.

One day we took the three-hour train trip to Lodz. I had asked my parents for their Lodz addresses. For the very first time, my mother gave me a handwritten family tree, providing the nicknames for her family members that I have used in this book. She also gave me the addresses of the apartments in which she and my father grew up.

We found my parents' homes easily my father's art deco apartment building across the street from the Museum of the Revolution, and my mother's apartment building now next door to a theater. But as soon as I arrived in Lodz I wanted to leave. At the time it was an extremely poor town, one that had lost its wealth and the textile industry for which it was famous. Anti-Semitism was still evident, even though there was only a handful of Jews left. We walked the deserted streets, which because of the grayness and poverty looked like the war had just ended, and fled back to Warsaw.

My parents barely asked me about the trip; they were not interested in seeing the photos of their still standing apartment buildings. I understood their silence. They had no desire to return to the places where they had lost everyone in their families.

The moment of hope that Solidarity epitomized was squelched shortly after our trip. My husband's colleague was imprisoned for his political activities and then died from a heart condition shortly after he was released from prison.

My second trip to Lodz took place in 2012, long after my parents had died. After reading the translated letters, I was ready to undertake a very different kind of visit one informed by the letters as well as by my growing understanding of Polish history. I was accompanied by my translator, Ela Gugula, a Polish university student fluent in English.

My impression of Lodz was very different than in 1981. Piotrkowska Street (or at least the part we visited) was chic. Stores and cafes lined the street, as did statues of famous Poles including Jews Izrael Poznanski the textile magnate, Artur Rubinstein seated and playing on a grand piano, and Julian Tuwim, a famous writer and poet of the interwar period. We visited a Jewish Community Center run by Orthodox Jews, who located my paternal grandfather's gravesite. We stayed in a lovely hotel built in the 1920s near Piotrkowksa Street. I felt that the city of Lodz was attempting to address the silence about the historic role of Jews in Poland, their numbers now reduced from over three million to a few hundred.

Although it is true that unlike in 1981 the Jews of Lodz were being honored, the changes sometimes felt "surfacey." When I wandered down side streets with old buildings that housed the poor, I could see anti-Semitic as well as other racist slogans on the walls. I learned that each year Lodz has a day in which citizens gather to remove racist and anti-Semitic graffiti, and I saw whitewashed evidence of those erasures.

When I visited the area of the Lodz Ghetto to find the street where my grandmother Mera lived, along with her sister Dora, Dora's husband Abram, and Abram's brothers, I noted the attempts at preservation of some buildings but also the failures. Painted markers on the streets to indicate the ghetto's boundaries were largely erased or hardly visible. I noted both the positive steps taken to memorialize the Jewish historical presence in the city as well as the continued anti-Semitism, even when there were no Jews to hate.

As my parents grew older, their losses haunted them. My mother, who died of Alzheimer's disease, lost her languages in the reverse order with which she learned them first English, then French, and finally when I visited, she greeted me only in Polish or Russian. And she called for her mother.

My father died shortly before his seventy-third birthday. It was a sudden death. He was working full-time but not feeling well. He went into the hospital and died three weeks afterwards. He was always a professed atheist, never attended a synagogue, and only among his closest friends from Poland, like Mark Zborowski, did he talk of the past. Nevertheless, when he was dying, he requested that he be buried in a Jewish cemetery. He had made no provision for this, but nearing death, he specified the cemetery in which he wanted to be buried and asked my husband and me to find a burial site for him and for my mother.

I do not know when and how my parents grieved when they learned of their family's fates. Their losses so great, the terrible news never ascertained with certainty until the end of the war, the impossibility of taking leave of loved ones, the cruelty and horror of their deaths left to the imagination and their need to move on and to create a new life took its toll on them. This must be true for all immigrants forced out of their country by war, racism, or poverty.

After my father died, I found thousands of carefully kept records of the patients he treated, often with operations that restored vision and hope. This was my parents' legacy and they worked at it with a devotion that people admired. Because they, unlike most of the others from their families, survived through an offer from Uncle Love, they were determined to make their lives worth living, and they did. Their history, and that of friends and relatives left behind, was carefully preserved in the carton, *Careful Old Letters*.

The label on the box is layered with more meanings than my parents could ever have imagined.

References

Adelson, Alan, and R. Lapides, eds. *Lodz Ghetto: Inside a Community Under Siege.* New York: Viking Penguin Books, 1989.

Clendinncn, Inga. *Reading the Holocaust.* Cambridge, UK: Cambridge University Press, 2002.

Davies, Norman. *God's Playground: A History of Poland, Vol. II: 1795 to the Present.* New York: Columbia University Press, 2005.

Dobroszycki, Lucjan, ed. *The Chronicle of the Lodz Ghetto 1941-1944.* New Haven: Yale University Press, 1984.

Eisenstein, Miriam. *Jewish Schools in Poland 1919-39.* New York: King's Crown Press, 1950.

Epstein, Julia. "Remember to Forget: The Problem of Traumatic Cultural Memory," in Julia Epstein and Lori Hope Lefkowitz, eds., *Shaping Losses: Cultural Memory and the Holocaust,* Chicago: University of Illinois Press, 2001.

Fox, Frank. "Mark Zborowski, the spy who came out of the Shtetl." *East European Jewish Afiairs* (1999), 119– 128.

Gross, Jan. *Fear: Anti-Semitism in Poland after Auschwitz: An Essay on Historical Interpretation.* Princeton: Random House, 2006.

Hartman, Geoffrey . *The Longest Shadow: In the Aftermath of the Holocaust.* Bloomington, IN: Indiana University Press, 1996.

Heller, Celia S. *On the Edge of Destruction: Jews of Poland between the Two World Wars.* Detroit: Wayne State University Press, 1994.

Hilberg, Raul, S. Staron, and J. Kermisz, eds. *The Warsaw Diary of Adam Czerniakow: Prelude to Doom.* Chicago: Ivan R. Dee, 1999.

Hoffman, Eva. *After Such Knowledge: Memory, History, and the Legacy of the Holocaust.* New York: PublicAffairs, Perseus Books Group, 2004. http://www.holocaustresearchproject.org/nazioccupation/to maszow-mazowiecki.html

Horwitz, Gordon J. *Ghettostadt: Lodz and the Making of a Nazi City.* Cambridge, MA: Harvard University Press, 2008.

Jackson, Julian. *The Fall of France: the Nazi Invasion of 1940.* Oxford: Oxford University Press, 2003. http://www.jewishgen.org/Yizkor/pinkas_poland/pol4_00154.html

Mishkinsky, Moshe. "The Communist Party of Poland and Jews," *The Jews of Poland Between Two World Wars.* Hanover, NH: University Press of New England, Brandeis University Press, 1989.

Mostowicz, Arnold. *With a Yellow Star and a Red Cross: A Doctor in the Lodz Ghetto.* Portland, OR: Valentine Mitchell, 2005.

Pagis, Dan. "Instructions for Crossing the Border," in Lawrence L. Langer, *Art from the Ashes.* New York: Oxford University Press, 1995.

Paxton, Robert. *Vichy France: Old Guard and New Order.* New York: Columbia University Press, 2001.

------. "Jews: How Vichy Made it Worse," *New York Review of Books* (March 6, 2014), 40–43.

Poznanski, Renee. *Jews in France During World War II.* Hanover, NH: University Press of New England, Brandeis University Press, 2001.

Rittner, Carol, and J. K. Roth. *Different Voices: Women and the Holocaust.* New York: Paragon House, 1991.

Rosbottom, Ronald C. *When Paris Went Dark: The City of Light under German Occupation 1940–1944.* Boston: Little Brown, 2014.

Rosenfeld, Oskar. *In the Beginning was the Ghetto: Notebooks from Lodz.* Evanston, IL: Northwestern University Press, 2002.

Sloan, Jacob, ed., trans. *Notes from the Warsaw Ghetto: The Journal of Emanuel Ringelblum.* New York: Schocken, 1974.

Trunk, Isaiah. *Lodz Ghetto: A History.* Roberto Moses Shapiro, ed., trans. Bloomington IN: Indiana University Press, 2006.

Zipperstein, Steven J. "Underground Man: The Curious Case of Mark Zborowski and the Writing of a Modern Jewish Classic," *Jewish Review of Books 2* (Summer 2010), 38–42.

Family Members

The Rozin Family

My mother Halina Rozin was born Lodz, Poland in 1908. She lived in Grenoble from 1928-30; in Paris from1932- 1939; and in Philadelphia from1938-1996.

My maternal grandmother Mera Kagan was born 1884 in Suwalki, Poland and died on September 28, 1942 in the Lodz Ghetto.
Dora Kagan her older sister was married to Abram Polakov. Dora's and Abram's son Arkadius (called Adek) Polakov probably died in the Warsaw Ghetto; he married Felicia Zerigyer, and they had a child named Anitka born in 1938, her fate is unknown.
Jacob Kagan, was Mera and Dora's much younger brother, who emigrated to the United States after WWI and settled in Chicago, where he practiced law. He changed his name to Jack Kanne in the U.S.

My maternal grandfather Alexander Rozin was born in Lodz 1882; he died in Lodz on December, 11 1938.
He and Mera Kagan married in January 1907.
He had eight siblings: those mentioned in the book include: Fredek, Janek, Artek, Pepa, Nunia, Tanya.

The Wolkowicz Family

My Father Michal Izrael Wolkowicz (spelled Michael in the U.S.) was born Lodz in 1910 and died in Philadelphia in 1983.
He lived and studied in Grenoble, 1928-30; became an ophthalmologist in Paris, 1930-38, and lived and practiced medicine in Philadelphia from 1938-1983.

My paternal grandfather Aron Wolkowicz, was born in Gombina, Poland, 1885; he married Roza Goldberg, who was born in 1889; both most probably perished in Treblinka, date unknown.

My father's first cousins who survived the war were Dosia (Dorota Wolkowicz) born in Lodz, 1922; Abram (known as Adek) Wolkowicz, born 1912 in Lodz. Both emigrated to the United States in 1947.

Acknowledgments

In addition to the outstanding translators, Elizabeth Kosakovska and Agnes McClure, who made this book possible, I would like to thank my editor, Rebecca McBride, for her wise suggestions and attention to detail and clarity.

I thank my husband, Sheldon (Shelly to me and our friends) Weinbaum who read my chapters in their various stages and encouraged me every step of the way. Because he is always direct and honest, I felt confidence to go forward with this project.

My parents who died many years before this book was written are nevertheless the inspiration for it. My father's foresight in keeping the letters, my mother's stories, which she related throughout my childhood, my many supportive and loving friends, and my children, Daniel and Alys Weinbaum, who encouraged me along the way, made this book possible.